The elegant pleasure gardens that were created behind the High Street houses of Newburyport during the mid-1800s were a horticultural landmark. When first built, they contained exciting new plants, cutting-edge designs, and delightful combinations of airy garden structures, stone paths, box *parterres*, luscious flower beds, beckoning views and shaded sitting areas. A century of gradual decline was followed by a civic movement to preserve and restore Newburyport's historic architecture, and there has been a parallel resurgence of interest in studying, renovating, and enjoying these designed outdoor spaces. Historic Gardens of Newburyport and Environs was formed to aid in this process. Our first project was to raise the funds to allow Lucinda Brockway of Past Designs in Kennebunk, Maine, to research the gardens of the Cushing House, home of the Historical Society of Old Newbury at 98 High Street. In the course of six years of fundraising Garden Symposia, Lucinda presented her lecture on Newburyport's High Street gardens. It was illustrated with slides of archival plans and photographs as well as modern images of remaining garden features. Her broad knowledge of landscape design history allowed her to follow threads from French *parterre* designs to the formal geometric beds you will see pictured in this book, and from William Perry's experience of his mother's High Street gardens to the appearance of some of the same design ideas in the restoration of Colonial Williamsburg. Lucinda's original lectures have been broadened by extensive additional research and expressive text by Lindsay Cavanagh, and by extraordinary photographs of the High Street gardens taken by Sally Chandler. This combination is enriched by generously shared family garden plans and photographs, Historical American Buildings Survey (HABS) plans of garden designs and structures drawn up in the 1930s, and the inclusion of several modern gardens in nineteenth century spaces, as well as an essay by Lucinda on what to do with a historical garden space if you are fortunate enough to have one. The original presentation, already generous in information, insights and graphic delights, has evolved into the book you now hold in your hands. We hope you will enjoy reading it as much as we have enjoyed creating it.

Stefanie Shattuck Hufnagel
President, Historic Gardens of Newburyport and Environs
*Newburyport, December 2003*

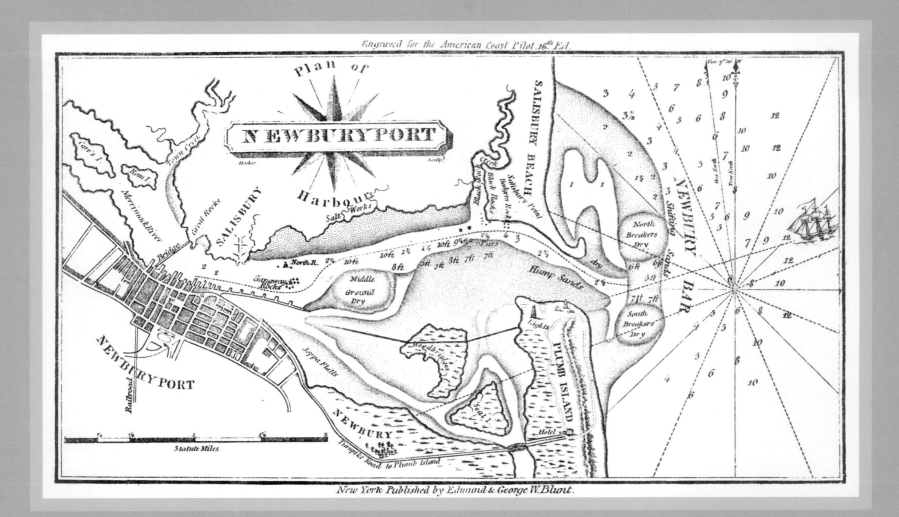

# GARDENS *of the* NEW REPUBLIC

*Fashioning the Landscapes of High Street*
*Newburyport, Massachusetts*

BY LUCINDA A. BROCKWAY AND LINDSAY H. CAVANAGH
PHOTOGRAPHY BY SALLY R. CHANDLER

**b**

**bright sky press**
Albany, Texas

*For Margie,*
*To a wonderful*
*gardener, my former*
*Point Planters partner!*
*Enjoy the book!*
*Love*
*Sally R. Chandler*

**bright sky press**

Box 416, Albany, Texas, 76430

10  9  8  7  6  5  4  3  2  1

**Library of Congress Cataloging-in-Publication Data**

Brockway, Lucinda, 1957–
　　Gardens of the new republic : fashioning the landscapes of High Street Newburyport Massachusetts / Lucinda Brockway and Lindsay Cavanagh ; photography by Sally R. Chandler.
　　　p. cm.
　　Includes bibliographical references (p. ).
　　ISBN 1-931721-41-6 (alk. paper)
　　1. Gardens—Massachusetts—Newburyport.  2. High Street (Newburyport, Mass.)  I. Cavanagh, Lindsay, 1936–  II. Title.

SB466.U65N7463 2004
712'.6'097445—dc22                                    2003069626

Book and cover design by Black Trout Design

Printed in China through Asia Pacific Offset

Front end paper: 63 High Street
End paper opposite page 1: 89 High Street
Portfolio photographs: Page 2: 47 High Street; Page 3: 98 High Street; Page 4: 67
　　High Street; Page 5: 89 High Street
End paper opposite page 160: Harriet Spofford's summerhouse on Deer Island
Back end paper: Atkinson Common

## d e d i c a t i o n

We dedicate this book to our parents, Robert and Sarah Shattuck, Eugene and Nancy Hooper, S. Avery and Elizabeth Raube. Their encouragement and example shaped our lives and made this garden history possible.

Stefanie Shattuck Hufnagel
Lindsay Hooper Cavanagh
Sally Raube Chandler
*Historic Gardens of Newburyport and Environs*

This book is dedicated to my parents, who cultivated seeds of independent creativity, to my husband who tends my everyday, and to our children, the fruits and flowers of tomorrow.

Lucinda Brockway
*Past Designs*

## acknowledgments

Our deepest thanks go to a remarkable generation of Newburyport women who shared with us their knowledge and memories of early Newburyport's gardens and their gardeners, including Ruth Burke, Lorna Learned, Wilhelmina and Sylvia Lunt, Esther Macomber, and Doris Rindler. Newburyport historians Greg Laing, Christopher Snow, and Jay Williamson shared their incomparable knowledge of area personalities and events, while Jane Carolan clarified the intricacies and evolution of Newburyport architecture. Karen Wakefield and the Newburyport City Improvement Society provided information about the Bartlet Mall. Current and former owners of the High Street gardens Clement Armstrong, Marc Cendron and Jennifer Day, Julia Farwell-Clay, Sue Heersink, Jerry Lischke, Bob Miller, Jenny and Ted Nelson, Maura and Bill Perkins and Jamie Yalla were generous with information, access, and photographs. Noted maritime author and professor Benjamin Labaree offered valuable advice, perspective, and encouragement. The use of paintings by local artists Lee Rowan, Jennifer Day, and Frances R. Morrill was appreciated, as well as the permission to use paintings from the collections of Dennis Radulski, Gayden Morrill, and Jim and Sally Chandler. Our thanks go to the Newburyport Garden Club for permitting us to use archival documents and photographs. The welcoming staff at the Hamilton Room of

the Newburyport Public Library made our work much easier, and Nancy Thurlow and other staff members of the Historical Society of Old Newbury were extremely helpful. Elizabeth Swanson of the Wheelwright House Board and Bev MacBurnie of the Belleville Improvement Society each shared their knowledge of and affection for their particular historic space. We are grateful to Lucinda Brockway, Jack Learned, Virginia Lowell, Elizabeth Singleton, and Christopher Snow for permitting us to use photographs from their personal collections. Lorna Condon, librarian at the Society for Preservation of New England Antiquities (SPNEA) was especially helpful. Special thanks also go to Jean Coughlin and Marc Page of Infocus for their invaluable technical photographic advice and service, to Carol Buckley for her careful copyediting, and to Penny Morrill for her encouragement.

*With special thanks to Robert and Sarah Shattuck*

# c o n t e n t s

PART ONE

*Fashioning the
High Street Gardens*

# FASHIONING THE
# HIGH STREET GARDENS

*Historian Samuel Eliot Morrison describes the affluent shipping community in* The Maritime History of Massachusetts: *"Newburyport boasted a society inferior to that of no other town upon the continent. Most of the leading families were but one generation removed from the plough or the forecastle; but they had acquired wealth before the revolution and conducted social matters with the grace and dignity of the old regime." That eighteenth century sense of distinction remains encapsulated today in the period houses carefully constructed along the old road that parallels Newburyport's hilltop ridge, separating it from the busy downtown. Despite the modern bustle, present day High Street retains the* grande dame *aura indigenous to the architectural and historic heritage of the city. Behind its tree-lined sidewalks, the old houses create a three dimensional textbook of American architecture.*

n Newburyport, Massachusetts, the rhythm of the fences and house fronts along High Street quickens and slows, marching to the beat of history. Many of these houses and their hidden gardens were designed and built when the new American Republic was in its infancy, struggling to establish cultural and economic independence. The three-story Federal mansions popular in New England's affluent coastal cities still dominate both sides of the street with their imposing size and confident insouciance. They are the long-lived results of Newburyport's early maritime fortunes and there is something compelling about their silent dominance of the High Street ridge. Today, each maintains its dignity and its privacy along the crowded thoroughfare; it is rare to catch even a glimpse of what lies behind their gates, in the gardens and the farthest recesses of the yard. The narrow street frontages, broad house façades, and lines of white wooden fences allow for only limited public viewing. Visitors must be received properly by the homeowner and then invited to pass into the heart of the property before seeing anything more. The Yankee sense of public propriety and private retreat is never more evident than along High Street in this New England village.

Architect William Perry, a High Street homeowner recognized for his work on the Rockefeller Foundation restoration of Williamsburg, Virginia, emphasized this air of preferred solitude in his description of High Street's nineteenth century Federal homes in his introduction to John Mead Howells' *The Architectural Heritage of the Merrimack.*

They form a line or community or group of houses over two miles in length possessing a composite air of dignified complacence. They resemble their cousins on the side streets, houses that are built closer to the street and to each other, but they bespeak an emancipation from congestion and an effort to bring into city life the amenities that are dependent on seclusion.

When guests are welcomed into the houses and behind the garden gates, a different world is revealed. Here are white-latticed nineteenth-century gazebos, well houses and summerhouses, intricate fences and geometric path systems, terraces, and a myriad of native and exotic plants. It is clear from their hidden location and from the overall design of their gardens that the surprise and pleasure found within these deep sunny spaces is for private enjoyment and not for public show.

In the pages that follow we will pass through some of those gates and glimpse a few of High Street's private garden spaces as they are now, and as they were during their well-documented heyday.

Newburyport is in northeastern Massachusetts. The town fronts the south shore of the Merrimack River where it runs into the Atlantic Ocean, and lies to the north of Boston and the old Cape Ann fishing communities. Its High Street follows a ridge of land running southwest of the river, and parallels it until curving south toward neighboring Rowley and Ipswich. Originally known as the County Road, it passed by scattered farmsteads, agricultural fields, and woodlands until the landscape began to change and become less rural in the 1800s. As in other New England water-oriented communities, Newburyport's early settlement took place along the active waterfront and expanded systematically, street by street, as the town grew. The steeper topography of the Newburyport ridge was one of the last areas to develop. The predominantly open land bordering High Street survived as a reminder of the rural character of the early town before urban expansion between 1800 and 1810 brought a rapid transformation. There was an unprecedented surge of construction that proceeded hand in hand with the destruction of established utilitarian buildings. The town's old barns and houses were either razed or moved to side streets as the tide of new construction reached High Street.

Although Newburyport's High Street houses and gardens are primarily associated with the nineteenth century, the story of the city begins much earlier, even before the colonial insurgents living along the eastern seaboard fought the British to gain their freedom. Typical of the young communities of the new Republic, Newburyport's early years were shaped by its strong ties to the Old World and by its unique experiences in the new. In New England, the early British colonial experience included a streak of the Puritan culture. This combination strongly influenced the Newburyport interpretation of the European Neoclassic architectural style later used in the construction of many of the High Street homes. Designs of the town's first pleasure gardens were similarly affected several decades later, in the 1830s and 1840s, although at that time primary influences were derived from the French landscape tradition.

In Newburyport, the gardens behind the High Street houses were not built during the same era as the houses. Typical Georgian or Federal style High Street homes constructed between the 1770s and the 1820s were built during the peak years of New England's maritime culture and epitomized the extraordinary success of merchants, sea captains and others who had cannily invested in the many profitable aspects of the West Indian and European trade. Decades later, the gardens built behind these houses were another badge of economic success, this time for men profiting from the new textile and shoe steam-powered manufacturing industries. Their interest in ornamental gardens reflected not only the accumulation of new and disposable wealth, but also a shift toward a more urban life; a fascination with new theories of horticulture and other natural sciences; and an ongoing interest, by members of the property-owning upper classes, in replicating the culture and fashions of Europe and the larger cities of Boston, New York, and Philadelphia.

*281 High Street.*

*From* The Mentor *magazine, 1916, 47 High Street.*

In addition, by the middle of the nineteenth century, some Newburyporters had joined the ranks of other wealthy and well-traveled New Englanders who were intrigued by the new developments in scientific exploration and lured by the social cachet of collecting unusual trees and plants.

As societal rules, norms, and demands shifted during the mid-nineteenth century, the role of the garden and its surrounding landscape changed. By the 1840s, self-styled social arbiters created a new proviso for those hoping to be included in their upper echelons—the ownership of a home set in an elegant and properly designed garden. Formerly, although there were flower gardens, domestic properties had been landscaped for practicality and necessity. Even families financially able to build on High Street needed grazing land for livestock and space for orchards, berry patches, and vegetable gardens. This strong emphasis on practicality shifted when the language of horticulture became part of the social lexicon. Although the former colonists adhered to European horticultural traditions, these were, of necessity, adapted to life in the new American environment. Adaptation was as true in domestic architectural design as it was in issues of horticulture, government and philosophy. The adaptive combination of old and new strongly influenced the Newburyport interpretation of the Neoclassic architectural style used in the construction of many of the High Street homes.

## The Houses

To fully understand the High Street gardens that emerged in the mid-1800s, it is important to look first at the houses they embellish, the properties that contain them, and the Newburyport economic and social structure that made their construction possible.

Yankee money, ingenuity, luck, and hard work built High Street. Its original homeowners were inspired by the opportunities of the new Republic, and enabled by the emerging financial rewards of an expanding maritime society. But, it is important to emphasize that the Federal landscape was a testament to hard physical work as well as to the American entrepreneurial spirit. Sweat from the labor of shipwrights and sailors, Russian miners, Canadian fishermen, and slaves from the West Indies, Africa, and the southern United States also made possible the construction of the houses and their gardens.

Although the names of sea captains, merchants and investors are remembered, the laborers who contributed indirectly to their economic success by creating the goods carried in Newburyport ships and sold by their merchants remain important components of its successful economic history.

By 1792, the national economy of the new Republic had recovered from the economic chaos and debts incurred by the Revolution. There was a remarkable surge of commercial growth. Between 1790 and 1807, New England prosperity was at its height, and Newburyport reaped its share of this financial well being. Maritime-based states were able to take full advantage of a series of wars between France and England, beginning in 1793, which gave merchants the opportunity for trade. Americans benefited from their country's status as a neutral nation, and it was especially advantageous in trade with France and the French West Indies. During that near twenty-year period, Newburyport's population grew to 7,643, a jump of 165% from its incorporation in 1764. During those prosperous years, hundreds of new buildings were erected throughout the town and the sophistication of the patterns of life was remarkable. In the middle of the twentieth century, Newburyport author John Marquand reflected on the style of that period in a 1940's brochure for a Newburyport Historical Society House Tour: "The elegance of the Newburyport Federal houses made a fitting frame for the life which was led inside them, surprisingly expansive and genial even when compared to present-day activities in Long Island, Bar Harbor or Newport."

With prosperity, Newburyport joined the ranks of a number of successful seaports along the New England coast. These communities—including Portland, Portsmouth, Salem, and Providence—had growing libraries, schools, and other cultural institution. As a result, they played an important part in the development of the Republic, serving as a combination market place and social center where people could exchange views and explore political thought, technology, science, and literature, as well as scout for new agricultural and commercial opportunities. Newburyport merchants had a keen eye for spotting investment potential. Six shipyards bordered the lower Merrimack River in the 1790s, and by 1793 local merchants owned and managed more than one hundred sailing vessels. Some Newburyport ships traded with northern Europe, but most sailed to

Puerto Rico and the islands of the West Indies where Merrimack Valley fish, lumber, bricks, and agricultural produce were swapped for sugar, coffee, and molasses. Other Newburyport ships profited from trade along the American and Canadian coasts. Foreign ports that had been closed to the English colonists opened to the new neutral trading Republic and this period of wide reaching trade and contact with the greater world ensured an ever-increasing sophistication as well as wealth in its merchant class.

Although there were fewer than 6000 people living in Newburyport at the end of the eighteenth century, its merchants reflected a high level of financial know-how. These men thought of their investments in federal as well as local terms—under their guidance, the town of Newburyport had been the first in the Republic to finance and build a warship for the newly created American Department of the Navy. Their letter, requesting federal consent, reveals their commitment to the Republic: "The inhabitants of this town at the present moment are animated with the most zealous resolution to support and defend with their lives and property, the government of their country, as well against the open attacks of foreign enemies as the insidious attempts of domestic traitors." The resulting ship, "Merrimack," built at the Federal shipyard in Newburyport, was launched on October 12, 1798.

Some of these same merchants had joined together in earlier years to buy, finance, and equip privateers; later, they contributed to the first stages of Newburyport's industrialization by combining to establish by corporate charter the Newburyport Woolen Manufactory and the Merrimack Bank. Visionaries, these merchants realized the importance of trade expansion to Newburyport's future success, and combined their capital to finance investments that would foster trade. These schemes included the Essex-Merrimack toll bridge to expedite the movement of New Hampshire goods to the Newburyport docks, a turnpike to link Newburyport with Boston, and incorporation of their group as The Proprietors of the Locks and Canals on the Merrimack River, to build a canal circumventing Chelmsford's Pawtucket Falls. They hoped a canal would improve opportunities for the lower river by simplifying the shipment of commodities from further inland to the river's mouth. Equally innovative was their establishment of the Newburyport Bank and the Newburyport Marine Insurance Company. Both offered important

*(Top) Newburyport Custom House, built in 1835. The classic structure was designed by Robert Mills. Mills, the first native trained American architect, built the United States Treasury building in Washington, D.C. during the following year.*
*(Bottom) The ship Merrimack, launched in Newburyport in 1798. Ninety-two feet long, thirty feet wide, and fifteen feet deep, the 355 ton vessel carried twenty cannons.*

underwriting opportunities and the means for entrepreneurs to preserve and grow their investment profits. Newburyport's Institution for Savings was "established solely for the encouragement of thrift, industry, and economy among the laboring classes." The financial

# Essex-Merrimack Bridge

The Essex-Merrimack Bridge, the first to cross the Merrimack River near the sea, was built in 1792 by Newburyport builder Timothy Palmer. Its design was revolutionary. Heavy timbers formed an arch that sat on two abutments, one on Deer Island's south shore, the other on the Newbury shore. (That area of town belonged to Newbury until 1851.) The northern half of the bridge connected the island to what was then the Salisbury shore and is now Amesbury. This section was a draw-bridge that sat on two abutments and three stone piers. The principles of construction used in this segment were new and used in several other bridges built by Palmer, who held the patents. Boatsmen complained that the southern half of the bridge was an obstruction to navigation, and it was replaced by a chain suspension bridge in 1810.

In February, 1827, owing to a weakness in the chains, the section between Deer Island and Newbury collapsed and fell into the river with a loaded team, two men, four oxen, and one horse. The horse and men were saved, but the oxen drowned. The bridge was soon repaired and reopened. In 1851, Newburyport established the bridge as a toll bridge. It remained a source of income until 1868 when Essex County commissioners declared it a public highway.

*Pastel by Francis Henry Richardson. Richardson (1859–1934) was the uncle of Frances Johnson, who lived at 203 High Street. He was a member of the Harcourt Studio in Boston, and painted with Celia Thaxter and Childe Hassam on the Isles of Shoals, off the coast of New Hampshire.*

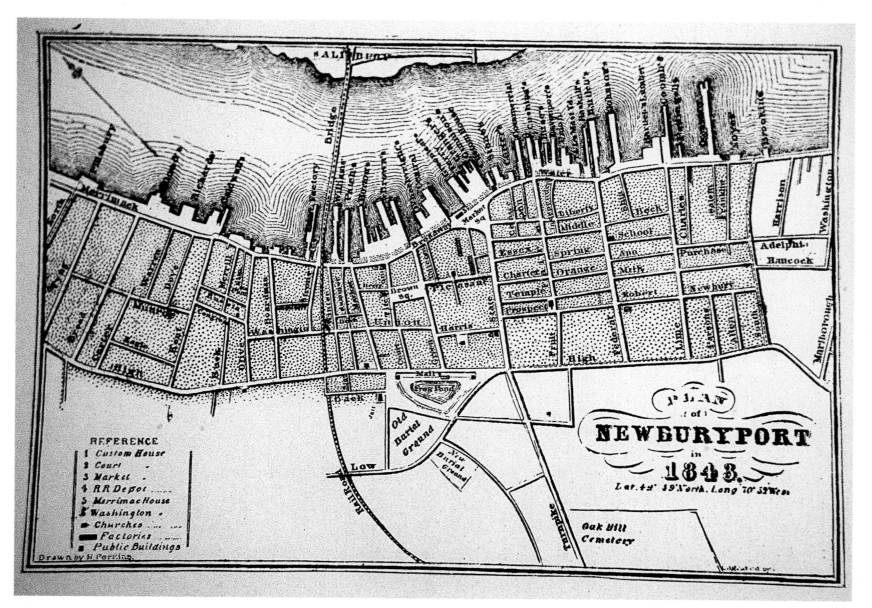

*1843 map of downtown Newburyport showing wharves and streets.*

base established by these men was an essential element of the town's long term economic growth.

When such men build new houses for their families, they require something special. Before the Revolutionary War, an expanding and prosperous population had turned to European pattern books and builder's manuals as their source for more fashionable building styles to replace the functional early New England colonial saltbox and other simple early period house designs. Gambrel, side gabled, or hipped roof English-style Georgian houses were the popular replacement in both the northern and southern American colonies. These styles remained dominant until the Revolutionary War, when building of all

kinds came to a near halt. Following the peace in 1783, the founding fathers turned to architecture as well as to the law for tools to aid in the difficult task of constructing a cohesive and permanent Republic. They were acutely aware of the necessity of creating a physical as well as a philosophical framework for their newly independent country. Some looked for inspiration to the simple, classic and noble principles of the early Roman Republic, with its philosophic ideal of public virtue and its architectural standards of elegance, balance, and symmetry.

At this time Neoclassicism based on Roman ideals was popular in Europe, and colonists who had traveled through France, Italy, and Germany felt at home with the concept of an American adaptation of

*(Top) First period house in Newbury, MA.*
*(Bottom) Typical Georgian colonial along High Street.*

European position that exposure to this style of architecture would elevate men's thinking to a plane of higher morality. Both spoke and wrote in favor of a consciously designed dignity in domestic and public architecture.

Builders also turned to the illustrations of classical antiquities discovered in the excavations of Pompeii and Herculaneum. Intact homes, buried and preserved for centuries under the ashes of the eruption of Mount Vesuvius in 79 AD, served as their inspiration for the Federal style. These archeological discoveries differed in their proportions from the Roman buildings that the Georgian style was based upon. Drawings and analyses of their measurements led to a new appreciation and understanding of geometric forms and of the underlying mechanics of the structure of the buildings.

Despite new influences, traditional Georgian architecture with slight variations remained the most commonly constructed style of building in both the southern and northern states during the early formative years of the Republic, and the designs chosen for both the President's House and the Houses of Congress in the new capital city of Washington were based on the English Georgian tradition. Georgian houses are also called Colonial as that style predates America's Revolution. Popular in England through the reigns of King George I, II, and III, the design was influenced by the architectural drawings of the Italian Andrea Palladio (1518–1580), who originated the use of the Palladian window still popular today. The Palladian window is an arched window flanked by two that are rectangular. Other common Georgian architectural details include triangular pediments or scrolls over the doorway; quoins, usually of faux-stone at the corners of the building; and large pilasters or columns emphasizing the façade.

Removed from the busy political hub of America, tradition-bound New England architects drew from Roman influences, but relied heavily for their interpretation on the writings and drawings of the Adam brothers, popular masters of English architecture. The brothers owned the largest architectural business in England at that time, and their illustrations of archeological antiquities did much to popularize the design elements of the Roman Republic. Robert Adam's enthusiasm for the arts of ancient Rome led to the replacement of the popular baroque-rococo Georgian architectural style by the calmer, more restrained Neoclassic. His delight in the delicacy of

the architecture of the Roman Republic for their own fledgling Republic. In turning to the Neoclassic form, the public adopted the popular western European romantic notion that architecture should embrace historic styles that enlightened, informed, and inspired humankind. American architects such as Thomas Jefferson and the influential English-born Benjamin Latrobe designed public and private buildings utilizing the classical early Roman style, and took the

Roman classicism strongly contributed to this shift in English and then in American architecture. His architectural pattern books included detailed designs of the decorative swags, urns, and garlands popular in Roman times that became standardized in simple rhythmic designs throughout the American Republic.

Neoclassicism, as it emerged in America, developed its own distinct characteristics. In its earliest forms, the Federal architectural adaptation combined old and new elements to create a spare and handsome style that differed only slightly from the earlier pre-war Georgian Baroque. The latter had incorporated flamboyancy and freedom in its designs, while Neoclassicism insisted upon an established system of independent parts joined in a comprehensive and rhythmic whole. Urban houses, such as those in Newburyport, retained their reliance on the traditional three-story Georgian English-style town house base, but made interior and exterior shifts toward Federal ornament, scale, and proportion. Many Newburyport houses appear to have 2½ stories, as the uppermost windows are smaller in size than the windows on the lower stories. Although there are indeed three stories in the Federal style houses, this ruse was used to circumvent the additional tax payments on a three-story house.

Designing and building houses of this magnitude required substantial skills. Professionally trained European engineers, mechanics, and architects who migrated to America following the Revolution brought with them a new level of building expertise that benefited and educated the former colonists. Despite this new technology, New England country architecture remained conservative and tied to the familiar. Life was primarily based on thoroughly British traditions and, despite the break with England, these patterns continued. Gradually, in addition to an awareness of the European archeological discoveries of Roman and Greek antiquities, influences expanding the narrow colonial mindset included a developing interest in French culture, and an appreciation of the new rationality-based architectural theories advanced in *Essai sur l'architecture* by the French Jesuit theoretician Marc-Antoine Laugier. Laugier attempted to demonstrate the logic behind building construction, arguing that building forms should be simple basic geometric units such as spheres, cubes and pyramids. These new ideas especially affected the thinking of architects and builders in the more sophisticated coastal communities.

*Type of Palladian window.*

Gradually, their work evolved beyond the prototypical Georgian styles of the colonials.

In New England, this evolution took the form of a basic cube shape combined with an exterior façade of balanced austerity. These two elements combined to set the tone of the sophisticated and understated Federal houses. The delicate and attenuated interpretation of this style by America's first native architects, Salem's Samuel McIntire and Boston's Charles Bulfinch, influenced architects, carpenters, and artisans constructing homes for the affluent mercantile aristocracy of other nearby New England seacoast towns. Bulfinch protégée Asher Benjamin joined others influencing styles in rural New England with the dissemination of his architectural pattern books for use by country builders. Benjamin's books, including *The Country Builder's Assistant* and *The American Builder's Companion*, were also popular throughout the new American states.

Use of the circle and the ellipse in both ornament and room plan typified the new style and contributed to its grace. Façades were symmetrical and gained their striking originality by proportion, win-

*Newburyport's old jail near the Bartlet Mall.*

dow position, decorative stringcourses and crowning balustrades. The focal point was the delicately carved front entrance, usually with a columned portico. Interior decoration was recognized for its refinement and delicate scale. Colors were muted. Geometric and natural motifs in varying sequences were used generously but in a constrained and precise manner. Like the chaste exterior, the interior mood was quiet and serene. The simplicity of style and the controlled reserve of the houses seems to reflect the strong Calvinistic streak that ran through the New England men-of-property building these houses. The success of Samuel McIntire, and his considerable influence on the Federal architectural style, may speak to the elegant restrained Puritan preferences of his clients, as well as to his skill with tools and wood.

Architectural plans for the handsome Newburyport houses are thought to be the products of local ships' carpenters, the anonymous artisans who built the graceful ships, brigs, and schooners that sailed from the city. The façades they built for the High Street Federal homes had a single flat plane and focused on the center entry. Decorative elements included the traditional graceful Palladian window, fanlighted entries without sidelights, porches supported by generally unfluted columns, and window caps with decorated entablatures. An entablature is made up of the decorative elements directly

above the window. Buildings designed and built in the town during the late eighteenth and early nineteenth centuries reveal both character and elegance, with Neoclassic design elements shaped by New England's early conservative colonial traditions. These houses do not incorporate the innovative details common to the ornate Federal houses of other affluent seacoast cities such as Portsmouth, New Hampshire and Salem, Massachusetts, where more elaborate façade designs include deep blind window arches and dramatic pilasters. This restraint has its own particular charm. But charm was nothing new to Newburyport. Even as early as 1800, before most of the High Street houses were built, Theologian and Yale College president Timothy Dwight described Newburyport in a highly appreciative manner: "[t]he houses, taken collectively, make a better appearance than those of any other town in New England…Indeed, an air of wealth, taste and elegance, is spread over this beautiful spot." This "air" can be directly attributed to Newburyport's post-Revolutionary War economic success, and the influence of classical design elements filtered through both European and American experience.

Although it had appeared that this success would continue indefinitely, both history and natural disasters combined to create a change in Newburyport fortunes after the near euphoric years that culminated in the construction of the High Street houses. A confluence of disasters checked the town's progress: locally, there was the emotional and economic devastation of a seventeen-acre major downtown fire in 1811, when over 250 buildings were destroyed and lay in smouldering ruins, and the uncertainties of shipping disruptions caused by the insidious silting in of the river bottom at the harbor's mouth; on a broader scale, renewed conflicts with England led to political problems, a shipping embargo, and eventually war. The prosperity that had flowed from European trade during the years of European wars ceased with the start of political wrangling with the English, who wished to stop neutral trade, and with the French who, as a tactic of war, hoped to stop all outside trade with England. The policy of foreign impressment of American seamen and the capture and cargo confiscation of neutral ships led to hard times for those dependent on maritime trades. In 1807, Thomas Jefferson's government responded to the conflict by clamping an embargo on all international trade to and from American ports in an effort to persuade the European opposition of the value of neutral commerce, and to avoid incidents that might spark a war. Not surprisingly, seacoast towns were against the embargo. In 1808, the *Newburyport Herald* reported: "There are now collected in our harbor 24 ships 28 brigs and 25 schs.—this is the first six months product of farmer Jefferson's embargo." A later article lamented: "Our wharves have now the stillness of the grave,—indeed nothing flourishes on them but vegetation." Jefferson's tactic proved ineffective, and the continuing discord led to the War of 1812–1815 with England. The main political effect of the war on the American Republic was isolation from Europe. In Newburyport, the economic effects of the Embargo and the war were profound. During the prosperous pre-Embargo years, the approximate annual value of exports leaving the Newburyport docks was $781,000. That figure plummeted to a wartime average of less than $12,000.

Save for Salem, Newburyport and its neighboring seaports lost most of their importance as major New England economic players following the end of the war in 1815. European waters and ports again opened to European ships, and American vessels no longer had a virtual monopoly in either the West Indies or Europe. At home, Boston had risen in the trading hierarchy to the further detriment of the smaller seaports. That growing city had gradually established links to a far-flung network of inland towns through a developing system of canals and roads. Trade goods from these towns were carried to warehouses on the Boston docks for export, and that city's expanding merchant class profited from buying opportunities with a myriad of small inland suppliers. In 1825, Caleb Cushing, High Street resident, Newburyport merchant, and the first United States commissioner to China, mourned, "Newburyport has withered under the influence of Boston." At the same time, foreign markets for New England goods declined sharply, because the same products could now be obtained closer to home in a newly peaceful Europe.

Townspeople continued to eke out a living: Newburyport's sizeable fishing fleet continued to sail; shipbuilding slowed but continued; the West Indian trade survived in a severely contracted form as did commerce with the eastern Canadian provinces. In 1815, the average wealth of the male voter fell to $2,716. Just seven years earlier, at the beginning of the Embargo, that figure was a healthy $5,089. Between the beginning of the enforcement of the Embargo in 1807, and the declaration of

peace in 1815, the number of wealthy Newburyport men with estates worth $25,000 or more fell from thirty-six to twelve, while those men worth $10,000 shrank from one hundred to sixty-two. So many local men were sentenced to terms in the Salem jail for bankruptcy that construction of a new jail in Newburyport was approved to keep families from being forced to make the long trek to Salem.

Few would find the resources to construct High Street homes during the second and third decades of the nineteenth century. Building limped to a halt. In Newburyport, although maritime and other small businesses continued to operate, there was a long difficult period before the shift toward a new industrial economy based on textile manufacturing began. High Street pleasure gardens would develop and prosper during this later period of change and new growth.

## The Gardens

In the 1830s, a new prosperity brought gardens to the fore following the long regional downturn. It had taken Newburyporters almost twenty years to regain sufficient confidence and capital to build again. There are always those profiting from change; some thrived in the new maritime carrying trade. As foreign markets for New England goods sharply declined after the war, local merchants who lost their established trading partners for New England products sent their ships instead to freight the southern cargoes that were still attractive to Europeans: tobacco, cotton, and flour. Captain John Newmarch Cushing freighted cargoes to Holland, Russia and the American northwest in his ever-increasing fleet of vessels, and eventually became the fifth wealthiest man in town. By 1835, there were thirty-two Newburyport ships enjoying considerable profits, and this number increased until the Civil War. The success of freighting led to the renewed expansion of Newburyport ship-building after its decline throughout the 1820s. In an August, 1822 article, the *Newburyport Herald* wrote: "The ship manufactory employs and supports more than thirty-two distinct trades, healthful in all its branches, and has been admirably calculated to nourish a race of active and hardy yeomanry." Sailmakers, blockmakers, ropemakers, and foundries remained busy; and the production of Newburyport rum, combs, chairs and soap continued. Despite these ongoing businesses and pockets of prosperity, most townspeople continued to struggle financially until the 1830s.

*Members of the Noyes family tending their garden in the early nineteenth century.*

shirting, and new buildings were constructed to house the growing population of factory labor. The Newburyport Steam Cotton Company built in 1836 was Essex County's first steam-powered textile mill and one of the earliest in the Republic. Aside from the textile mills, Newburyport's established cordage, hosiery, and comb factories became newly steam-powered. The traditional standbys of shipbuilding and cod and mackerel fishing complemented the town's new mills and workshops. By 1840, the Newburyport economy was finally again in a positive cycle. Even the fishermen were thriving. In 1847, 4,200 shad were taken by seine in one haul at the river's mouth. By 1851, ninety fishing vessels owned by Newburyporters were at sea. Currier's *History of Newburyport, Massachusetts* reports close to a thousand men employed as fishermen.

The horticultural consequence of the affluence that rewarded Newburyport's mid-nineteenth century manufacturing success included the addition of pleasure gardens and ornamentals to what had been strictly utilitarian landscapes. Gardening was certainly not a new activity. Domestic agriculture was essential in the colonies and there had been a lucrative business in the commercial importation of European grasses, fruit trees, and vegetables to the New World since the 1600s, and at the same time, unfamiliar specimens from America had been shipped back to Europe. By 1830, there was a distancing from physical agricultural labor by members of the upper classes. One offshoot of this distancing was a new horticultural professionalism. Gardeners, nurserymen, horticultural writers, and garden advisors took on new importance. Another change was the introduction of ornamentals to areas traditionally devoted only to vegetables. This departure from tradition was not always well received. In her 1879 memoirs, Newburyport native Sarah Anna Emery recalled her grandmother's defense of the decision to cultivate flowers:

Grandmam' took great pleasure in her flowers. Though sister Noyes 'could not see how she found time for sich fiddle-dedes,' and brother John's wife pronounced 'sich things all vanity,' and other wise people thought it would be better to raise something useful, grandmam' continued to cultivate her garden to the end of her long life...She considered flowers of great value. The Almighty had decked the whole universe

Real growth rode on the back of the textile industry. Newburyport's revival came in the late 1830s and 1840s, when power fueled by coal-generated steam engines made an industrialized textile business profitable. Trade and manufacturing was helped by the extension of the old Eastern Railroad to Newburyport. This was added to in 1849, with the construction of a line to Haverhill that connected with the Boston and Maine. But times had changed; unlike the earlier years of the Republic, when any man with brains, luck, and energy could make his fortune in the maritime trades, the textile industries offered real entrepreneurial opportunities only to people who already had capital to invest. Downtown, the face of Newburyport changed as large brick millyards were built to manufacture cotton sheeting and with beauty, Who was not made happier and better by pretty surroundings? For her part she considered every woman's duty to make her home as agreeable as possible. She was sure her good sisters-in-law and the other croakers enjoyed a bunch of pinks or a rose, as much as anyone, and her mints and sweet herbs were in great demand, especially lavender, to strew in drawers amongst linen.

The New England interest in ornamental horticulture in the 1830s reflected the drift of the population away from the farming base traditional to the colonies and the young Republic, toward a non-agricultural town life that was seen to offer more possibilities to the region's farm-grown youth. Growing numbers of people with extra time and money brought a new interest in things not essential, and so the popularity of pleasure gardening expanded. It was a new concept. Until that time, most larger properties had consisted of a service area near the house for laundry, a small "necessary" house, a well, a simple flower and herb garden, a vegetable garden, an orchard and berry patch, a poultry yard, and enclosed pasture land for the family cow and horse. Now, a greater proportion of the property would be devoted to planting beds designed with beauty and enjoyment in mind.

Paralleling the pressures pushing townspeople toward creation of a pleasure garden, a movement developed to improve society through general beautification of the home landscape. This trend was popularized in tandem with other movements to improve the general population through temperance, prison reform, missionary work, and general benevolence. A well-cared-for public or domestic landscape became a means to measure the level of refinement, industry, and even the intelligence of a family, or a community. Because of the upper class separation from gardening as work, the concept of ownership of an ornamental garden could be romanticized, and as the movement toward beautification implied, a garden's care and development could be viewed as an instructional or even a spiritual activity. An example of the educational aspect of this beautification movement was the Newburyport Horticultural Society, established in 1832 to foster an increased awareness of horticulture, botany, and landscape design.

Seedsmen seconded these new dictums in garden books and articles. In *The New American Gardener*, Thomas G. Fessenden described

*Caleb Cushing, United States Envoy* extraordinaire *and owner of 63 High Street.*

ornamental gardening in 1830 as "one of the most innocent, the most healthy, and to some the most pleasing employment in life," while in his book, *The Flower Garden*, Boston seedsman Joseph Breck was of the opinion that women and gardening were especially suited:

The cultivation of flowers appears more suited to females than to man. They resemble them in their fragility, beauty, and perishable nature. The Mimosa may be likened to a pure-minded and delicate woman, who shrinks from even the breath of contamination; and who if assailed too rudely by the finger of scorn and reproach, will wither and die from the shock.

In Newburyport, the prosperous citizen was not entirely focused on the redemptive nature of ornamental gardening. There was prob-

# Newbury-port Horticultural Society

Many nineteenth century New Englanders delighted in horticultural competition. Formal exhibitions gave gardeners an opportunity to show off their special plants, rarities, imports, and dried and fresh flower arrangements. A small cracked-leather-bound book with a gilt design and title announcing Newbury-port Horticultural Society reveals the minutes of a once-active society formed in April, 1833, under the leadership of Ebenezer Moseley. "A meeting of Gentlemen friendly to the formation of a Horticultural Society in Newburyport and vicinity was held this day at the office of Ebenezer Moseley Esq." Five officers and ten trustees led the group, and seventy men signed the minute book as Society members. Fading Spencerian script reports the events of annual meetings from 1833 through 1836. Although the minutes end, unpublished papers in the archives of the Historical Society of Old Newbury state that the Society continued to hold many exhibitions each year for twenty years, when interest in membership appears to have faded. The first horticultural exhibition was held on September 19, 1833. The list of award winners illustrates the plant diversity and extent of exotic introductions found in Newburyport homes and gardens during the 1830s. Some of the Society awards were won by: Miss Lydia Brown, fig tree in full fruit; Miss Lydia Bartlett, South American plant—sea rattles; Mrs. R. Atkins, vine from Havana; Miss Hodges, several species of geraniums, dahlias, coreopsis, and a noble hydrangea....

In an age when men still dominated the horticultural, botanical, and scientific farming societies, the women of High Street were recognized for their own horticultural endeavors. A few days after the 1833 exhibition, an article was reprinted in the local paper from the *Boston Transcript*: "Among the contributors to the first exhibition of the Horticultural Society of Newburyport we noted with pleasure the names of no less than six ladies. It is rare to find the name of any lady attached to fruit or flowers in the rooms of the Boston Horticultural Society." This distinction may represent one of the earliest examples of public recognition for women given in New England.

In an exhibition held on July 26, 1834, entries from more than three dozen gardens vied for recognition. Among the many mentioned in the *Newburyport Herald* were: Miss Hannah Frothingham, Chinese primrose, japonica and liner leaved celsia; Captain Edmund Bartlet, India plant; Mrs. G.W. Coffin, Calcedonia, sedum, and a three foot acacia in full bloom, Miss Huse, smoke tree and Mrs. Prout, pomegranate. That October, the exhibition featured house plants, fruits, and vegetables. Among the entries were a gold dust plant and a caper tree as well as citrus and figs.

The following minutes of the Newburyport Horticultural Society were taken by "Thos. B. White, Recording Sec'y."

## Saturday, September 7, 1833

The exhibition of fruits, flowers and vegetables this day in the room over Mr. Morss' store on State Street, was highly creditable to the Society and to the town and vicinity—The Society is very much indebted to the Ladies, who so generously assisted in arranging the tables and displaying the various productions—The day was fine. There [were] many strangers present among whom was the Hon. John Quincy Adams—Ex President of the United States, all of whom expressed themselves well pleased with the exhibition.

## Thursday, October 2, 1834

Owing to the absence of many of the officers of the Society on the 13th of September when the annual exhibition would have been held, it was postponed until this day when an exhibition was had at Phoenix Hall unsurpassed by any former one of the Society and perhaps, considering the many disadvantages under which the Society labours and the very great advantages enjoyed by our neighbors in Boston—not surpassed even by them.

The Society then sat down to a very extensive water mellon and a musk mellon of a most exquisite flavor raised by and presented to the Society by their worthy president to which together with a Bottle of very superior wine furnished by Mr. W. Osgood, ample notice was paid and the Society separated highly gratified with their entertainment.

In 1906, long after the Horticultural Society held its last exhibition and its membership faded away, a group of ladies including Mrs. M.S. Bernheimer, Mrs. C. F. Perry, and Miss Margaret Cushing attempted to revive the tradition of the Newburyport Horticultural Society to benefit the grounds of the High School. Among the many varied plants entered in this exhibition, Mrs. James Hale offered a very rare passion flower; Reynold Dodge, well-known botanist and author of a standard book on ferns, put in a collection of showy lady slippers, ferns, and other wild flowers; and Mrs. Bernheimer and Miss Cushing submitted rare and unusual roses. The entry of Mrs. Harriet Spofford of Deer Island, a poet, was choice mixed flowers and a branch from a very old pine. At that time the pines were estimated to be more than 400 years old and had been used as the subject of poems by both Mrs. Spofford and her friend John Greenleaf Whittier.

*Nathaniel Tracy. Although Tracy's twenty-four privateers wreaked havoc among the British fleet, only one of these ships still survived by the end of the Revolutionary War. Tracy also suffered heavy losses from investing in the Continental bonds that helped to finance the Revolution. These bonds were not redeemed at face value until years later when Alexander Hamilton established the Bank of the United States in 1791. Needing money, Tracy settled earlier for far less. He was forced to sell his State Street property and moved to Newbury where he died. In 1787, Alice Tucker, spinster daughter of Newbury's First Parish Church pastor, commented in her journal about Nathaniel Tracy's fate: "He shone for awhile and attracted the notice of the admiring multitude but now is overshadowed and sunk into obscurity, many are disposed to compassionate him, but the World in general are too ill natured to bestow such a soothing consolation."*

*Gardens of Colony and State reports that George Heussler, an Alsatian gardener brought from Europe to tend the Tracy garden, was fired when Tracy's fortunes turned. Heussler writes that his employer "cast the poor stranger unpaid upon the world." Under his care, Tracy's orchard annually produced 140 bushels of plums, pears, apples, cherries, and peaches. Moving to Salem, Heussler improved his position; he was soon placed in charge of the splendid Derby gardens. Both in Salem and Newburyport, Heussler was the first professional gardener with both an education and practical training.*

ably a strong element of the social imperative in Newburyport in the 1830s and 1840s, as there had been in the 1770s, when merchant *extraordinaire* Nathaniel Tracy demonstrated his personal wealth and power in the construction of a formal garden and large orchard adjacent to his brick Federal mansion in the heart of downtown Newburyport. (Tracy's former home is now incorporated into Newburyport's expanded public library.) Almost a century later, successful businessmen tapped into the same vigorous force that motivated Tracy, when they redesigned their extensive properties for the inclusion of an enlarged garden. By the mid-nineteenth century, the concept of pleasure gardens had become a normal aspect of life for the upper and middle classes. Well-traveled Americans visited gardens in European aristocratic homes, strolled down formal garden

paths in America's larger urban centers, and had access to popular horticultural journals and books that discussed the development of ornamental gardens on the continent.

Influenced by publications, well-traveled friends, and personal impressions of European gardens, Newburyport home owners constructing their new gardens chose the traditional French design despite the opinion of the American influential horticulturist-turned-architect Andrew Jackson Downing, who accused the "ancient" or geometric French style of association with the style of autocratic societies and royalty, and therefore judged it not fitting for use in the United States where "the rights of man are held to be equal." Tensions between Republican ideals and French design notwithstanding, the simple French style of geometric garden beds was adopted as the garden design of choice by upper and middle class trend-setters both in New England and New France.

This turn toward France was doubtlessly strengthened during the aftermath of the War of 1812 when the former colonists attempted to distance themselves from their traditional ties to England. Despite the bad feelings resulting from Napoleon's policies toward neutral shipping, French influence had always been strong in Newburyport, dating back to the American Revolution and to the visits of the French patriot and American revolutionary hero the Marquis de Lafayette and other Frenchmen who supported the American Revolutionary cause. At the close of the eighteenth century, this New England corner of the Federalist world had been strongly influenced by an admiration and emulation of all things French. In the early years of the Republic, political theories of the *philosophes*, Voltaire, Diderot and Montesquieu, had been read and discussed; high-waisted gowns in the style of the French *haut monde* had bedecked the ladies; Napoleonic Empire furnishings still graced the parlor; and French-inspired decorative arts and aesthetics continued to pervade the American psyche. It is not surprising to find French design influences later in the garden as well.

Some in the upper levels of Newburyport society would have had personal experience of France and its design tradition. For people with the status of Caroline and Caleb Cushing, a visit to European gardens would have been *de rigueur*. In France, the geometric garden tradition established initially by André Le Nôtre at Vaux-le-Vicomte and Versailles in the seventeenth century had remained popular. In England, structured formality had been replaced in the eighteenth century by a more natural and romantic landscape style fostered by English landscape gardener and architect Lancelot (Capability) Brown. Those building the High Street gardens in Newburyport were influenced by both of these traditions, but the structural principles of French design predominated throughout the Republic. Terraces, walks, and geometric garden beds crisply delineated their spatial purpose and tamed the natural landscape into a newly ordered formality.

The Newburyport gardens constructed between 1830 and 1850— which could be identified as a Federal style although appearing much later than the Federal period—offer a significant contribution to this largely unstudied garden and landscape design period. In present day horticultural circles, landscape historians tend to neglect the mid-century French influences in American gardens due to their preoccupation with a search for English influences in the period precedent to the Victorian gardening extravaganza. It is interesting to consider these gardens not as precursors to Victoriana, but as a natural response of the New England temperament to a certain clarity and discipline found in the French garden style. This preference harks back to the region's earlier connection with the austere yet refined Neoclassic Federal building style. The pleasure gardens of High Street seem to have evolved as a natural philosophic partnership between house and landscape.

## Patterns of the High Street Gardens

Newburyport's gardens conformed to the major precepts of French design, despite vernacular exceptions, but adopted some characteristics of English design as well. Their restrained yet highly geometric patterns showed no inclination to the natural or picturesque demands of English gardens of the day. In Newburyport, parterre beds were carefully edged with clipped boxwood or other small hedges and borders, in a manner similar to the classic gardens of Versailles. In a bow to the English style, the interior of the garden beds was luxuriantly planted with colorful varieties of popular nineteenth century perennials and annuals: roses, Canterbury bells, larkspur, iris, bachelor buttons, campanula, and monkshood. In the traditional French garden, bed interiors would have been grass or colored gravel, keeping the focus off the individual bed and on the overall geometry.

Although the properties on High Street are complete residential landscapes, with utilitarian as well as ornamental plantings, they are referred to within this book as gardens. All are introverted in their outlook, well hidden from both the street and their neighbors. Each represents a highly diverse collection of plants, set within a strict geometric design. Each long slender property is subdivided into terraces for flowers, fruits, and vegetables that are carefully linked in a clear progression of aesthetics and utility. The intimacy and detailing found in each property combine to create a cloistered garden, surrounded by buildings and fences. As "guarded yards," these landscapes are really highly defined gardens. Although each is unique in its contents and detailing, there is a distinctly common pattern of similarities among them.

Each property has a narrow street frontage and elongated rear yard. This village subdivision pattern is typical of seacoast New England communities, including Providence, Newport, Salem and Portsmouth. Property was divided into narrow, long lots, fronting on the road and river. With at least a 100 foot street frontage, lots provided street and water access, and maximized the total number of lots related to the village core. Where lots did not run to the water, private lanes or tertiary roads provided service access to the rear. This configuration offered maximum privacy from the street because the house spanned the width of the lot, hiding the rear yard from public view. As such, the trees, hedges and gardens behind the house were separated from the streetscape, and the public way became a highly architectural passage. Bands of shade trees, planted in "tree belts" at the edge of the public way, offered pedestrians the only opportunity for shade and greenery, until mid-century Victorian homes were situated to allow for front yard plantings which contributed to the public way.

The largest properties were located on the south or higher side of High Street, with some south-facing terraced rear yards falling down the back side of the High Street ridge. The grounds of the High Street properties were designed with a flower garden and/or "pleasure yard" near the house, leading down to another narrow terrace for a fruit garden or orchard, and then down again to a vegetable garden and pasture. In a few cases, the topography caused the order to be reversed, with the serviceable plantings high on the ridge and the pleasure yards stepped down to the rear of the house.

Properties on the north or river side of High Street, closer to Newburyport center, were smaller and not as distinctly terraced. These properties did not have the advantage of space or strong vertical variation in topography. They were, however, just as highly ornamented and compartmentalized as their neighbors across the street. They maintained more spacious lots than homes closer to the village center, sometimes combining two lots into one. High board fences and hedges provided the same privacy for family space and separated the house yards from the public view.

Many of the properties have a long history of family ownership. In many cases, High Street properties have continuously passed from one generation to another, in contrast to other New England communities, more remote and less adaptable to changing economic trends, that have watched younger generations move away from the family homestead. Those that have changed family ownership have often sold to owners who retained the original garden design. Newburyport's adaptable economy and proximity to Boston, first by boat or coach, next by rail, then by automobile, allowed this continuity. With each new generation of homeowners, the High Street houses were updated to reflect improvements in household comforts, and the garden contents were changed to reflect period preferences in plants and in color combinations. Overall, however, the architectural styling and landscape designs were changed very little. Clearly, these families respected tradition and reflected Yankee thrift.

Many properties were designed as double houses, though they appear as very large single family homes. A number of High Street homes built in the early nineteenth century were designed with a central front door, central hall, and regular symmetrical room arrangement. Side doors were added to both side façades, connected by a cross-axial hallway. Often, if the property was divided, these side doors became the main door to each house, with the front door serving merely ornamental purposes. The central hall became the dividing line for family ownership, and the lot lines followed the central hall out the rear door to the rear of the property, creating two very narrow long lots. Deed research reveals a consistent combining and subdividing of the house along these lines, offering a very flexible system for splitting and recombining property as family fortunes ebbed and flowed or children equally split their family inheritance.

Both house and grounds were adaptable enough to have retained their integrity for 150 to 200 years. There are examples where this is not the case, but a large number of these "Federal" gardens retained their integrity because the houses could easily be subdivided and recombined as they passed from one generation to the next. The lot sizes were adequate and not so large that they were a tax burden to the homeowner; if land was sold, the terraced design allowed acreage to the rear to be sold along with it, keeping the remaining garden design unaffected by the change. Newburyport's location and adapting economy offered opportunity for homeowners to obtain income adequate enough to maintain their properties; garden designs were not overwhelming, were easy to understand and were possible to maintain, though they required a significant amount of hand labor. When and if they were simplified, they often retained the structure of the original design, minus the intensity of the floral contents.

A significant number of High Street houses were built between 1800 and 1811, the year the Newburyport waterfront was irreparably damaged by fire. Between 1790 and 1811, Newburyport saw an unbridled growth in its residential community. Much of High Street was built up during this period. The 1811 waterfront fire, the economic disruption of the War of 1812 with the resulting impact on Newburyport's diminished economy, and the silting of the harbor combined to end significant new construction. After 1830, as the industrial opportunities in Newburyport revived its fortunes and the train connected the waterfront city to Salem and Boston in 1840, the burgeoning economy spawned a new era of growth and expansion, at which time residential architecture experimented with the strikingly different emerging Victorian styles. The Federalist era which created Timothy Dwight's "air of wealth, taste, and elegance" was over. But its ornamentation with formal pleasure gardens was just beginning.

*In the pages that follow we will visit some of the High Street gardens that resulted from the economic resurgence in the mid-nineteenth century. Many are presently in various stages of repair and rejuvenation. Sadly, others have almost vanished. The properties are listed both geographically and by their historical development. Many of the gardens have parallel histories. Some had more important developments later in the nineteenth and twentieth centuries, but these changes often reinterpreted the aesthetic details of the earlier gardens.*

*Illustration of the change of level along the High Street ridge. The garden structures are both functional and ornamental. Clockwise from upper left, garden structures at 63 High Street, 79 High Street, 75 High Street, and 47 High Street.*

PART TWO

*High Street Gardens*

# INTRODUCTION

Soon after the founding of the new Republic, Newburyport became one of the most successful ports on the Atlantic seaboard, reaching its pinnacle of maritime economic activity in the early 1800s, when most of the High Street houses were built. The thriving mercantile center fell into the first of its periods of economic dormancy shortly afterwards, remaining depressed until mid-century when the invention of the steam engine revived its fortunes. The new stream of profits financed construction of the European-style gardens that were built behind the 'grand old ladies' of High Street.

## CONSTRUCTION DATES OF
## THE HIGH STREET HOUSES AND THEIR GARDENS

| | HOUSE | GARDEN | ADDRESS |
|---|---|---|---|
| Pierce Perry Healy Yalla | 1809 | 1815 | 47 High Street |
| Pike Cushing Burnhome | 1810 | c 1881 (1920) | 63 High Street |
| Stocker Wheelwright | 1797 – 1836 | 1840s | 75 High Street |
| Wheelwright Richardson | 1810 | unknown | 77 High Street |
| Livermore Lunt Barron Dobson | 1803 – 1805 | post 1838 | 79 High Street |
| Osgood Brockway | 1807 | 1842 | 83 – 85 High Street |
| Greenleaf Wood Perkins | 1799 | Modern | 87 High Street |
| The Moulton House | 1800 | c 1840 | 89 – 91 High Street |
| The Cushing House | 1818 | c 1830 | 98 High Street |
| Moss Learned Nelson | 1805 | 1840s | 190 High Street |
| Jackson Dexter Kelley Quill | 1774 | c 1780 | 201 High Street |
| Lowell Tracy Johnson Farwell-Clay | 1774 | 1774, 2001 | 203 High Street |
| Mount Rural | c 1780 | 1780 | 241 High Street |
| Miltmore Husk Heersink | 1809 | 1920s | 281 High Street |

From their beginnings, Newburyport's High Street homes and gardens have provided the backdrop for fêtes, soirees, and extravaganzas. As a sense of community obligation grew in the Republic, High Street residents rallied, opening their homes for events that would benefit a wide range of social causes. A balloon ascension at Mt. Rural raised interest and money for the city's Griffin Home for Aged Men across from Atkinson Common. Members of the Garden Club hosted horticultural exhibits to fund landscaping for the new High School in the 1930s. During both World Wars, elegant garden parties brought in dollars for the Red Cross, and over the decades, house tours benefited local museums and private schools. In 1979 the Historical Society of Old Newbury began its tradition of June Garden Tours, offering the public a rare opportunity to look behind the fence and walk through the latticed gates of Newburyport's historic gardens.

## 47 High Street
# PIERCE PERRY HEALY YALLA HOUSE

broad, slightly pink old-brick walk and a welcoming curve in the handsome fence invite visitors to the door of one of the most photographed homes on High Street. Captain Benjamin Pierce bought the property in 1809, and it remained in that family until it was bought in 1898 by Georgianna Graves Perry. The house construction was complete by 1812, and is quite similar to the Moulton house at 89–91 High Street. The interior is especially noted for its original drawing room wallpapers that tell the story of Telemachus, the son of Odysseus. These papers, like the papers in the dining room of the Miltmore Husk Heersink house and several others in Newburyport, were made by the famous Parisian firm of Dufour and Leroy between 1812 and 1827.

According to the Historic American Buildings Survey (HABS) researchers, the garden was laid out in 1815. Dates mentioned in this survey were not always accurate as they were based on oral history as well as archival evidence. The garden probably dates to the 1830s, as do many of the other High Street gardens. This property differs from the others on that side of High Street as the topography rises above the house, instead of falling off the ridge to the rear as it does in the houses further along the street. The buildings—house, barn, and lean-to—conceal the extensive grounds from the street. The pleasure garden *parterres* originally sat behind the house, on the lowest terrace. Above this garden, accessed via a small set of wooden steps, extended a broader cutting garden and fruit garden. The vegetable garden was on the uppermost terrace. Arborvitae, roses, and other shrubs hedged the front of each level, creating more intimacy by screening the contents. A long central path bisected each terrace and served as the connecting spine through the length of the entire garden. The *parterre* gardens were designed as a series of long rectangular beds on the east side of the axial path and a pattern of an ellipse-within-a-rectangle west of the path. At the top of the uppermost terrace sat a latticed, vine-covered arbor. This upper terrace was less formal, and offered magnificent views of downtown Newburyport, the Merrimack River, and Plum Island.

Mrs. Georgianna Graves Perry purchased the property in 1898. Her family came from Newburyport, and presumably she returned there after the death of her husband to raise her children. Her original family home lay directly across the street. At the time of her purchase, William Graves Perry, her eldest son, who would later gain fame through his work in the restoration of Williamsburg, Virginia, was fifteen. Between 1901 and 1905 he attended Harvard College, so his years in Newburyport were limited, but he was clearly drawn to the city as his architectural career developed. In 1921 he received the commission to

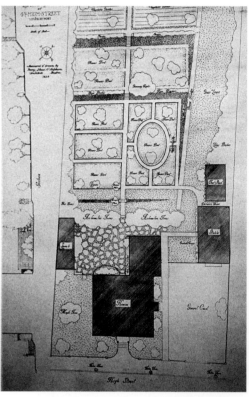

*A recently replaced garden arch frames a view of the house.*

and gardeners of the American colonies and the Republic that members believed were important before 1840. Between 1927 and 1935 the bulk of Perry's architectural work focused on the restoration of Colonial Williamsburg. This work for the Rockefeller Foundation guaranteed his architectural reputation. In 1936, he returned to Newburyport when he inherited his mother's house after her death. In the following years, he summered in Newburyport and spent the remainder of the year in Boston. The significance of William Perry's link to Newburyport, and in particular his connection to the recognition of the historic significance of the High Street properties, has only begun to be investigated. He can be credited with documenting some of these gardens in 1924, for restoring the summer house at the Cushing House in 1934, and for the more complete documentation of the High Street properties under the HABS program during the depression years, where he served on the advisory committee. In addition, Perry worked tirelessly with preservationist William Sumner Appleton to save many of Newburyport's colonial period houses that were directly in the path of the Route 1 bypass built in the 1930s and 1940s. Some of these houses were moved to other sites, while others were simply destroyed.

Today, only the basic structure of the original garden remains on the property. The latticed arbor and most of the wooden steps deteriorated under the shade and moisture of the trees which slowly came to dominate the garden terraces. The central path in the garden remains along with some of the boxwood borders. Much of the former pleasure garden is devoted to open space for family sports: soccer and baseball. The current owners have recently restored the house, its outbuildings, and its intricately designed fence. New garden structures—arbors and a summerhouse—have been constructed, their new design carefully incorporating the sheaf-of-wheat pattern featured in the fence and the roof balustrade.

Despite the elimination of its original garden, two unique particulars lend this property special interest to landscape historians. First is its well-documented connection to the long legacy of French-inspired High Street gardens; and second is the connection of the property, through the efforts of its owners, Georgianna Perry and her famous son, William Graves Perry, to the first stirrings of the twentieth century preservation movement.

design a new St. Paul's Church on High Street after a fire devastated the historic wooden church. In 1924 he documented two of the High Street gardens (the Moseley garden at 182 High Street and his family house at 47 High Street) for his mother, who served as chair of the Historic Gardens Committee for Newburyport and wrote much of the Newburyport text for *Gardens of Colony and State*. This book, commissioned by the Garden Club of America, described gardens

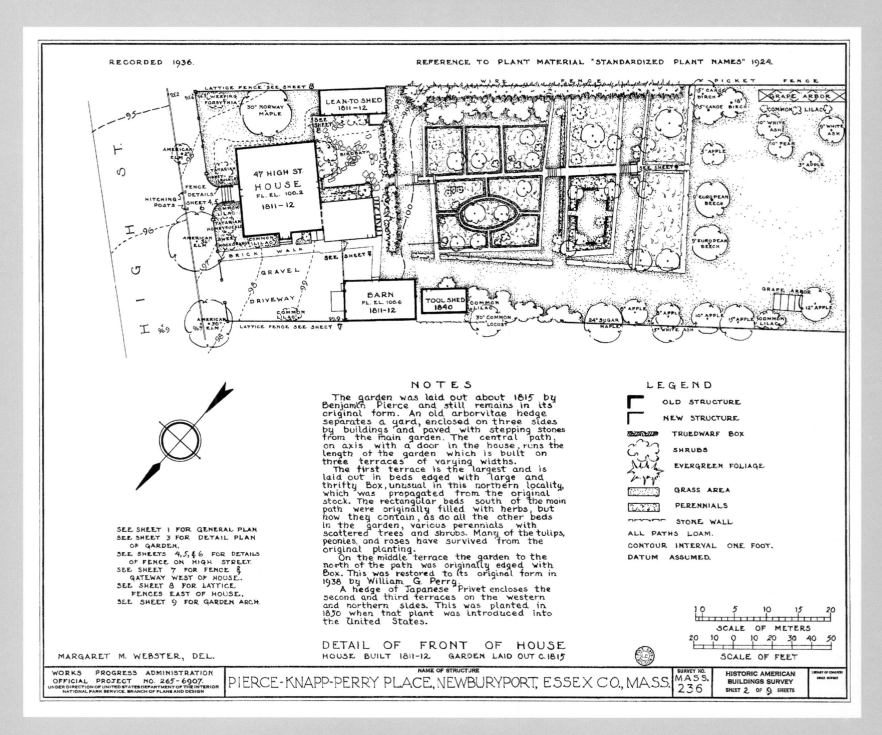

RECORDED 1936.  REFERENCE TO PLANT MATERIAL "STANDARDIZED PLANT NAMES" 1924.

NOTES

The garden was laid out about 1815 by Benjamin Pierce and still remains in its original form. An old arborvitae hedge separates a yard, enclosed on three sides by buildings and paved with stepping stones from the main garden. The central path, on axis with a door in the house, runs the length of the garden which is built on three terraces of varying widths.

The first terrace is the largest and is laid out in beds edged with large and thrifty Box, unusual in this northern locality, which was propagated from the original stock. The rectangular beds south of the main path were originally filled with herbs, but now they contain, as do all the other beds in the garden, various perennials with scattered trees and shrubs. Many of the tulips, peonies, and roses have survived from the original planting.

On the middle terrace the garden to the north of the path was originally edged with Box. This was restored to its original form in 1938 by William G. Perry.

A hedge of Japanese Privet encloses the second and third terraces on the western and northern sides. This was planted in 1850 when that plant was introduced into the United States.

LEGEND

OLD STRUCTURE
NEW STRUCTURE
TRUEDWARF BOX
SHRUBS
EVERGREEN FOLIAGE
GRASS AREA
PERENNIALS
STONE WALL
ALL PATHS LOAM.
CONTOUR INTERVAL ONE FOOT.
DATUM ASSUMED.

SEE SHEET 1 FOR GENERAL PLAN
SEE SHEET 3 FOR DETAIL PLAN OF GARDEN.
SEE SHEETS 4, 5, & 6 FOR DETAILS OF FENCE ON HIGH STREET.
SEE SHEET 7 FOR FENCE & GATEWAY WEST OF HOUSE.
SEE SHEET 8 FOR LATTICE FENCES EAST OF HOUSE.
SEE SHEET 9 FOR GARDEN ARCH.

SCALE OF METERS
SCALE OF FEET

MARGARET M. WEBSTER, DEL.

DETAIL OF FRONT OF HOUSE
HOUSE BUILT 1811-12    GARDEN LAID OUT C.1815

WORKS PROGRESS ADMINISTRATION OFFICIAL PROJECT NO. 265-6907. UNDER DIRECTION OF UNITED STATES DEPARTMENT OF THE INTERIOR NATIONAL PARK SERVICE. BRANCH OF PLANS AND DESIGN | NAME OF STRUCTURE  PIERCE-KNAPP-PERRY PLACE, NEWBURYPORT, ESSEX CO., MASS. | SURVEY NO. MASS. 236 | HISTORIC AMERICAN BUILDINGS SURVEY SHEET 2 OF 9 SHEETS

*Historic American Buildings Survey (HABS) drawing. These drawings, made in the 1930s, are part of the collection found in the Library of Congress.*

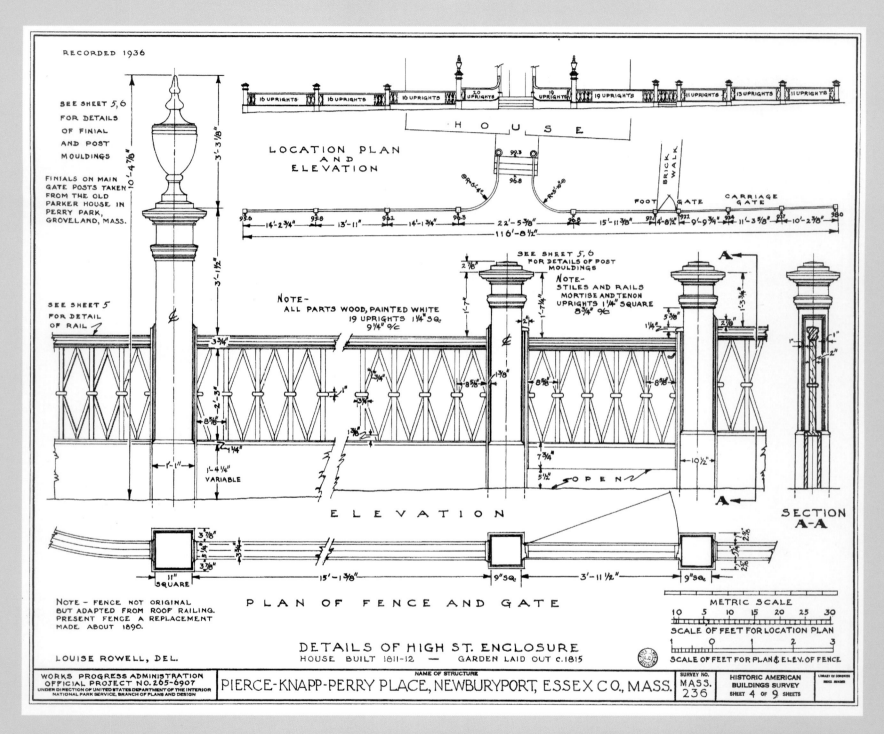

RECORDED 1936

SEE SHEET 5,6 FOR DETAILS OF FINIAL AND POST MOULDINGS

FINIALS ON MAIN GATE POSTS TAKEN FROM THE OLD PARKER HOUSE IN PERRY PARK, GROVELAND, MASS.

SEE SHEET 5 FOR DETAIL OF RAIL

LOCATION PLAN AND ELEVATION

H O U S E

16 UPRIGHTS · 16 UPRIGHTS · 16 UPRIGHTS · 20 UPRIGHTS · UPRIGHT 19 · 19 UPRIGHTS · 11 UPRIGHTS · 13 UPRIGHTS · 11 UPRIGHTS

BRICK WALK

FOOT GATE          CARRIAGE GATE

14'-2¾"   13'-11"   14'-1¾"   22'-5⅞"   15'-11⅜"   4'-8½"   9'-9¾"   11'-3⅝"   10'-2⅜"

116'-8½"

SEE SHEET 5,6 FOR DETAILS OF POST MOULDINGS

NOTE - STILES AND RAILS MORTISE AND TENON UPRIGHTS 1¼" SQUARE 8¾" ℅

NOTE - ALL PARTS WOOD, PAINTED WHITE 19 UPRIGHTS 1¼"SQ. 9¼" ℅

A

O P E N

A

SECTION A-A

E L E V A T I O N

NOTE-FENCE NOT ORIGINAL BUT ADAPTED FROM ROOF RAILING. PRESENT FENCE A REPLACEMENT MADE ABOUT 1890.

LOUISE ROWELL, DEL.

11" SQUARE        15'-1⅜"        9"SQ.        3'-11½"        9"SQ.

P L A N   O F   F E N C E   A N D   G A T E

METRIC SCALE
10   5   10   15   20   25   30
SCALE OF FEET FOR LOCATION PLAN

1   0   1   2   3
SCALE OF FEET FOR PLAN & ELEV. OF FENCE

DETAILS OF HIGH ST. ENCLOSURE
HOUSE BUILT 1811-12  —  GARDEN LAID OUT c.1815

WORKS PROGRESS ADMINISTRATION
OFFICIAL PROJECT NO. 265-6907
UNDER DIRECTION OF UNITED STATES DEPARTMENT OF THE INTERIOR
NATIONAL PARK SERVICE, BRANCH OF PLANS AND DESIGN

NAME OF STRUCTURE
PIERCE-KNAPP-PERRY PLACE, NEWBURYPORT, ESSEX CO., MASS.

SURVEY NO.
MASS.
236

HISTORIC AMERICAN BUILDINGS SURVEY
SHEET 4 OF 9 SHEETS

LIBRARY OF CONGRESS

*(Opposite page clockwise from top) William Graves House, 56 High Street, the childhood-home of William Perry's mother Georgianna Graves Perry. William Graves Perry, lead architect Colonial Williamsburg, Principal of Boston architectural firm Perry, Shaw, and Hepburn, and designer of Saint Paul's Church, 166 High Street. Photo of Graves summer-house, presently dismantled. Detail of new garden structure built by craftsman Dean Sheehan follows the design found in the fence and roof balustrade at 47 High Street.*

*Two early views of the garden. (Inset) Photograph from 1916,* The Mentor.

# Elements of French Landscape Design

Every style of American landscape design has key elements that define and characterize that style. The characteristics of the early nineteenth century American gardens are their transition from the rigid formality of the eighteenth century to the irregular naturalistic designs of the later nineteenth century. In effect, these gardens are highly structured spaces that utilize the basic principles of classic French landscapes, but they are planted with colorful masses of perennials and flowering shrubs favored by English gardeners. Landscape historian Norman Newton identifies several key elements of design that characterize the ideal French landscape. Many of these elements reveal themselves in the Federal gardens of Newburyport, Massachusetts. According to Newton, there are seven basic checkpoints for the true French garden:

**Structure in spatial geometry.** The High Street gardens are highly structured, featuring geometric garden beds, rectilinear terraces, and carefully contrived uses of three-dimensional space.

**A structured plan.** Clearly, these gardens have highly structured plans and carefully delineated and prioritized uses of space.

**Central or radiating paths.** Most of the long, narrow High Street lots prevent the use of the grand *pate d'oie*, or goose foot, arrangement of paths radiating from a central point. The limited scale of the High Street gardens does not allow for multiple path systems. However, the circulation through these garden spaces features central paths that bisect the yards, creating a linear spine for the garden. From this central path, secondary paths lead to the garden boundaries, follow the edge for a short distance, and return to the central path via another path.

**Crisp edges.** The boxwood hedges lining the garden paths and the use of fences, arbors, and hedges all combine to create the crisply defined lines of these nineteenth century gardens. Fences—picket, lattice and

board—strictly frame the narrow lots and clearly define property edges. Terraces and walks create a clear delineation of spatial purpose and tame the natural topography into more ordered formality. Arbors and other architectural features define transition points from one level to another and serve as four-season sentries within the ever-changing moods of the garden.

Walks with controlled edges using trees or hedges. All the gardens feature boxwood-edged paths and garden beds. This use of low evergreen hedges, often only six inches high, creates a crisp edge to the paths, and a three-dimensional appeal to the garden. The boxwood reinforces the geometry of the garden, preventing the colorful contents of the beds from spilling over onto the paths, and creates a multi-season appeal to the garden. In those gardens where boxwood was not used as an edging feature, paths and beds are defined by deeply cut ditch edges, lines of low perennials, or the crisp line of path material, usually brick or stone.

Projecting horizontal space in design and vegetation. The varied and narrow topography of the gardens limits the expansive use of the horizontal plane. However, the highly defined lines of the terraces emphasize the horizontal rather than the vertical components of the property. The broad expanse of yard near the house, with its intricate horizontal patterns, reinforces the sense of expansive space within the garden, and the limited use of large, over-story trees and shrubs emphasizes the more prominent horizontal rather than vertical elements within the garden.

The contents of the flower beds reflect a more traditional English use of plant material. Colorful flower beds of perennials, annuals, and roses were more often located in the *potager*, or kitchen garden than in the formal *parterre* in traditional French design. In the Newburyport gardens, these plants interrupt the clean lines of the geometric beds with their colorful blooms and their height (sometimes 4–6 feet taller than the boxwood hedges). The horizontal projection of spaces is interrupted during the summer season by the contents of the beds and is rediscovered each autumn when cold weather puts an end to the blooming season.

Sheets of geometrically formed flat water. This is one element of the French garden that did not translate into the Newburyport version. The use of water is non-existent in these gardens. The only examples are found where the household well is located near the house, or the well and watering troughs are located in the pasture at the far end of the property. These water elements are utilitarian, rather than aesthetic. In all cases, the High Street properties do not abut the

Merrimack River where the element of a naturally occurring water feature could be celebrated in the design of the garden.

Wide sets of stairs. Like the element of water, wide sets of steps are not featured in the High Street gardens. Instead, the paths are rather narrow by French standards—three to four feet wide as compared to the broad promenades featured in formal French gardens. Stairs within the garden are only as wide as the paths, yet they are most often located along the central spine of the garden, and often associated with a piece of garden architecture, such as a summerhouse or arbor, to emphasize the change in grade.

Panels of turf between walls or hedges. The use of turf in these gardens is very limited or nonexistent. Expensive to develop and maintain, turf was featured only in gardens of the well-to-do. Panels of lawn did ornament small portions of the pleasure yards and *parterres*, but were not used between walls and hedges. More often, these turf areas were dedicated to outdoor sitting and to games, particularly for croquet later in the nineteenth century.

Views and vistas defined by the *clair voyée* (grill opening) to outward views, long paths through woods, and carved stone urns or statues at important crossings. This is one of the more interesting aspects of the French garden translated into American use. All of these gardens had carefully controlled views and vistas. Their narrow spaces and introverted designs did not feature broad views to the larger landscape as was typical of the principles of French design. Instead, arbors and summerhouses created *clair voyée* opportunities to view portions of the garden as if looking through a window or door opening. Long paths through the garden were emphasized in the overall design. Though these paths did not travel through woods, they did travel between lines of tall flowering shrubs, beside parterre garden beds, through terraces of orchard trees, and over, under, and through garden steps, summerhouses, arbors, and bowers. Carved stone urns or statues were not featured in the American versions, but certainly the positioning and use of the summerhouse, arbor, and other architectural features filled the same purpose as the stone urn or statue in the French garden.

Clearly these Federal gardens of High Street are a tribute to the French philosophy of geometric principles and carefully controlled garden design. Though perhaps not as democratic in philosophy as landscape designer Andrew Jackson Downing would have preferred, these gardens and their contents separated the merchants of High Street from their less wealthy neighbors. The size of their lots, the size of their houses, and the contrived arrangement of their private garden spaces set them apart from the rest of the town, where crowded smaller lots were dominated by simpler colonial homes that jostled for position with their outbuildings and their neighbors. These smaller properties left little room for garden splendor, and no opportunity to establish their owner's social status in the eyes of the general public that passed by their doors.

The properties on High Street left no doubt about the social status and refined aesthetic tastes of their owners. These men emulated the garden designs of Europe and the architectural influences of antiquity in creating the physical realization of the new American Republican ideals. Classical studies were the foundation of a good education in the New Republic. Buildings featured columns or pilasters of the four classical orders. Buildings like the Parthenon, the Pantheon, and the Colosseum of Rome provided unlimited sources of architectural inspiration for the private homes and public buildings of the United States Republic. Similarly, Italian villa gardens, such as those of the Villa Medici or Villa Farnese, celebrated the formality of the parterre. One definition of *parterre* is 'to divide the ground.' In France, Le Notre's design for Vaux le Vicomte, the famous gardens of Versailles, and even the gardens of Lafayette offered design inspiration for the well-connected American traveler. When Caleb and Caroline Cushing took their honeymoon tour of France in the 1820s, their letters and diaries are rich with references to gardens they visited, from the promenades of Paris to the grounds of Lafayette's country chateau. From Maine to Florida, the East Coast was replete with homes and gardens modeled on the symmetrical, formal designs of Italy, France, and England popular in Europe in the eighteenth century and before.

It is hard for us to imagine this passion for symmetry and formality. The gardens of High Street were crafted during an era before the natural, the sublime, the picturesque and the beautiful—the vocabulary of the English Landscape School—had crossed the Atlantic. Mount Auburn Cemetery was barely conceived. Neither was New York's Central Park nor Boston's Emerald Necklace. The brush strokes of the Hudson River School of painters were still damp on their canvases. We were a nation of scientific farmers, merchants,

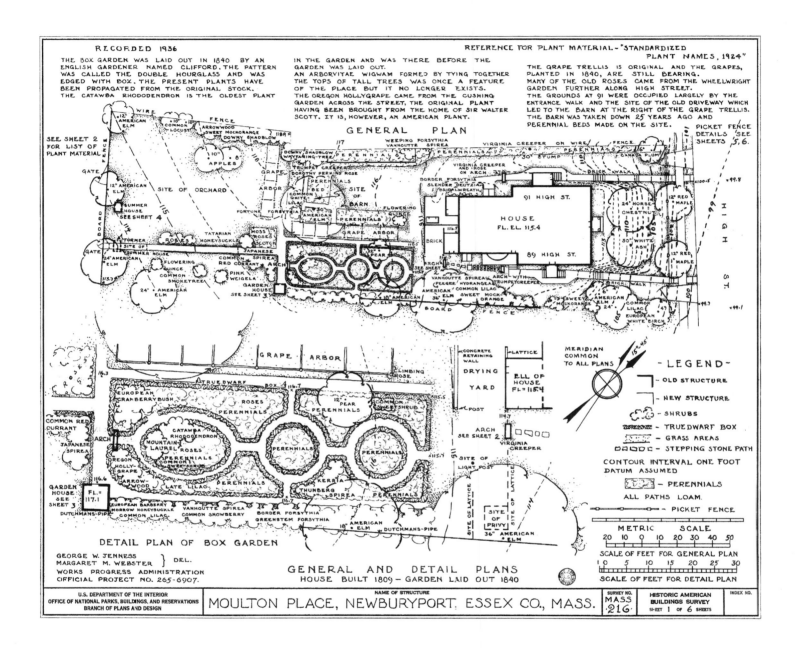

industrialists, and frontiersmen. "Cultivated," "highly manicured," and "highly fashionable" were the landscape ideals of the day. No one could imagine a backyard of green lawns, barbecues, and outdoor patios. Nature was suspect, and the wilderness something to be kept at bay: not to be celebrated but to be tamed.

Americans inherited a rich tradition in both horticulture and design from the French—perhaps it can be considered their "gift" to the emerging Republic. The early years of the nineteenth century featured French fashion, furniture, and decorative arts. In the city of Washington, the plan for the nation's capitol, conceived in 1791 by French architect Pierre L'Enfant, was in its early phases of construction. Hybridized Belgian and French pears, apples, and cherries were the pride of New England orchards and the subject of horticultural books and articles. And perhaps one of our richest landscape treasures, town gardens, such as those built along High Street in Newburyport, stemmed from one of France's greatest gifts to the Republic: the gift of inspiration.

## 63 High Street
# PIKE CUSHING BURNHOME HOUSE

Newburyport merchant Richard Pike purchased the gently rolling property on the upland side of High Street and constructed a large, handsome and comfortable Federal house for his family in 1810. An important figure in Newburyport, Pike was one of the founders of the Newburyport Academy at 85 High Street as well as an incorporater of the Marine Insurance Company founded in 1799. By the 1830s, ownership of the house had passed to Caleb Cushing who lived there briefly with his wife, Caroline Wilde Cushing, following their marriage in 1824. After her death in 1832 at age 28, Cushing spent much of the year in Washington and Boston fulfilling his growing political and legal obligations, although he did maintain his ownership of the property for many years. A Newburyport favorite son, Cushing went on to serve as United States Attorney General under President Pierce, as well as the first United States Envoy *extraordinaire* and Minister Plenipotentiary to China, where he negotiated the opening of Chinese ports for American trade. Returning to Newburyport at mid-century, Cushing became a judge of the Massachusetts Supreme Court and was elected mayor of Newburyport.

Little is known of Caleb Cushing's garden, although he and his wife had traveled to France on their honeymoon and, according to tradition, returned from there with a garden plan. In 1887, Soloman Bachman and his wife purchased the property as a summer home and enlarged it with the purchase of a meadow and other land behind the original lot. Extensive fruit, flower, and woodland gardens were developed during the decades of ownership of the Bachmans and their daughter, Mrs. Caroline B. Burnhome.

Their turn-of-the-century gardens featured flowering shrubs, perennials, and a wide collection of unusual nineteenth century trees. During the early Bachman years, unpublished Newburyport papers mention that the head gardener and his six assistants planted and tended 40,000 plants in the garden beds. Even if this is an exaggeration, the numbers hint at the vast scale of their horticultural efforts. Both Bachman and his daughter developed high style Victorian gardens on the property which post-date most of the other gardens along the street. The landscape overflowed with flowers, shrubs, and the newer plant materials imported to America from the Far East. Interest in exotic trees and shrubs ran high in the late nineteenth and early twentieth century, fostered by a new interest in exploration. Charles Sprague Sargent's influence at Boston's Arboretum encouraged plant collectors such as Ernest "Chinese" Wilson to travel the world in search of plants for the Arboretum grounds. Some of these exotic plants have naturalized happily in the woods

*1917 garden party at the Burnhome estate to benefit the Red Cross.*

behind the Pike Cushing Burnhome house and in the adjacent property and still survive today. These include Kentucky coffee trees, various Japanese maples, and an Halesia or silver bell tree

Reputedly, the most spectacular of the Burnhome high-Victorian, bedded-out gardens was in front of the house. The design for a round bed near the house began with a border of yellow coleus, followed by circles of flowering geraniums centered with tall crimson canna. The driveway was flanked by a palm-leaf shaped bed filled with various colored coleus plants. Opposite the door on the northwest side of the house was a bed of canna and caladium, some with leaves over a yard long. Urns overflowing with cascading flowering plants were placed at regular intervals on the walks throughout the property. Long herbaceous borders flanked the back walk leading to the summer-

house. At one time the borders held deep red coleus, General Grant and Miss Gertrude geraniums, achyanthus, and lobelias. A large rose bed featured rare imported varieties. During the lifetime of Mr. and Mrs. Bachman the property was open to the public two days a week to benefit charities. Their daughter continued this tradition, often holding garden fetes and fairs in the garden during World War I for the benefit of Britain and the allies.

When the property was put up for sale in 1945 by the estate of Mrs. Burnhome, it still retained its horticultural appeal. The realtor's description emphasized that "The grounds about it have an unusually wide variety of trees and shrubbery, while an established lawn surrounds the residence on three sides. A secluded rear terrace of old brick tiles overlooking the lawn and garden has exceptional appeal…The winding driveway leads to a side entrance and to the barn-garage in the rear, while a country lane runs further back, passing large flower and vegetable gardens and terminating at the two-acre meadow. There are an established rose garden, rock garden, perennial border, grape arbor and an interesting wooded hill…Outbuildings include the barn-garage for four cars with four cow tie-ups, box stall and room and lavatory above, heated greenhouse, tool house and old summer house." Many aspects of the extensive inventory of the Burnhome property could have applied to almost every one of the houses along High Street. Their unadorned and well-kept barns and carriage houses continue to remind owners of the 19th century need for utility as well as pleasure.

Today, most of the garden plantings are gone, but the brick stairs and terraces remain, as do the masses of rhododendrons that edged the garden. Trees planted in the nineteenth century have naturalized themselves through the edges of the woods and within the gardens and yards of the property. The land was subdivided after 1945, and the barn-garage area converted to another private residence. The main house was divided into apartments. Remnants of the vegetable garden remain, including some of its service structures and fences. So do the sturdiest of the plantings and the garden features. Although photographic images are all that remain of the garden, the haunting atmosphere of the Bachman garden ruins remains in the woods behind the house, and it is easy to imagine Caroline and Caleb Cushing entertaining friends in the parlor of the massive Federal house.

## Morrill Place
### 209 High Street

The Hoyt Morrill House was built in 1806 by Captain William Hoyt. From 1836 until 1862, the house was owned by Henry Kinsman, a Boston attorney and law partner of Daniel Webster, who was a frequent overnight guest. The home passed through a number of owners before it was purchased in 1897 by Frank Forrest Morrill. It remained in the Morrill family until 1978 when it was again sold and converted to the Morrill Place Inn Bed and Breakfast.

On November 23, 1824, while Judge Samuel Wilde occupied the Hoyt Morrill House, his daughter Caroline Elizabeth Wilde married Caleb Cushing in the house parlor. The marriage was performed by the Reverend John Andrews, then pastor of the First Religious Society of Newburyport. The new bride moved down the street to 63 High to take up residence and begin her married life.

On a fine day in 1947, the members of the Newburyport Garden Club gathered for a group photo. Standing, back row, left to right: Rosamund Snow, Katherine Dodge, Suzanne Little, Rev. Glen Tilley Morse, Gertrude Husk, Nellie Connolly, Rita Little, Alice Higgins, Edith Kinsman, Ruth Connolly Burke, Helen Learned, Florence Hale, Jane Everett Graves, Mabel Hale, Nell Todd, Ellen Graves, Elizabeth Brown, Jennie Upton Jones. Seated, middle row: Margaret Cushing, Helen Moseley, Peggy Morrill Wilkens, Margaret Dodge Morrill, Kathryn Morris Learned, Florence Bushee, Mary Wilding White, Conzuella Clark, Gerry Bullard, Eleanor Eames. Seated on the ground: Nancy Noyes, Jeanette Peirce, Nancy Stone, Alice Burke, Helen Lawton, Mary Atchley.

The rose-covered summerhouse at 63 High Street was the inspiration for the Newburyport Garden Club logo drawn by Laura Coombs Hills in 1930. Ms. Hills, a garden club member, was known for her miniature portraits on ivory and her floral pastels. Several of these are in the Museum of Fine Arts, Boston.

## 75 High Street
# STOCKER WHEELWRIGHT HOUSE

The property at 75 High Street contains one of the best surviving authentic examples of Federal style gardens in Newburyport. The square three-story Federal house fronting the garden was built by Captain Ebenezer Stocker around 1797, and is similar in its basic design to its nearby neighbor at 79 High Street, the Livermore Lunt Barron Dobson house. An old pump house, originally shared with 73 High Street, continues to provide an architectural grace note to the border area of the Stocker Wheelwright pleasure yard. Many of the homes on the ridge still have gates or spaces in their borders that allow homeowners to pass through hedges, walls, or fences to visit the adjoining backyard.

Between 1808 and 1826, the property changed hands four times; Ann Adams, who later married her cousin, John Wheelwright, was the fourth owner. In 1841 the property passed to William Wheelwright. A prototype entrepreneur and adventurer, Wheelwright made his name and a considerable fortune in South American shipping and railroads. In 1835, he established a steamship line carrying passengers and cargo between Chili, Peru, and the Panamanian Isthmus. As Wheelwright was away a good deal more than he was in Newburyport, he offered the Newburyport house to his parents, Ebenezer and Anna, for their residence, with his two sisters, Susan and Elizabeth. The property remained in the Wheelwright family until 1888, when it was transferred by deed of gift from William's widow Martha to a popular Newburyport cause: the Society for the Relief of Aged and Indigent Females. Today, over a century later, it remains owned and operated by this organization as a rest home for older women who enjoy its homelike character.

The garden was designed by Henry V. Ward, a personal friend of William Wheelwright, and planted by a Newburyport gardener who is referred to in notes only as "Armstrong." Later, Wheelwright employed an English gardener, Thomas Caper, to tend the formal garden. Caper worked for the Wheelwrights in this capacity for more than thirty years. William Wheelwright enjoyed flowers and plants, especially the aesthetic qualities of the *parterres* with their varied fragrances, varieties of plant shape, and combinations of color.

According to the Historic American Buildings Survey (HABS) documentation of the garden, the barn for the house was relocated in 1886, after the change of ownership, from a site immediately behind the house to the site of the greenhouse, which was removed.

*Circa 1860 photograph by Philip Coombs. On top of the summerhouse spire was a small scale model of the Old South Church in Newburyport. The model is gone but much of the garden layout remains the same.*

Later, a new wing was built onto the rear of the house, leaving only half of the original garden pattern.

The earliest surviving photograph of the garden dates to the 1860s. This photograph is unique, because it depicts members of the family and an individual believed to be the gardener, leaning over to more closely examine one of the flower beds. Photographs of these gardens are rare for the nineteenth century and photographs of gardeners are almost non-existent.

The garden follows the typical High Street layout with its long narrow shape terraced to fit the descending contours of the land. A pleasure yard was laid out immediately behind the house on the highest terrace level, a plateau that contains the house, lawn, and flower gardens. It was accessed directly through the rear door of the dwelling and was in a direct line with the front door. In the original Wheelwright design, garden beds outlined in boxwood formed a Maltese Cross. Between the arms of the cross lay small circular beds, also edged with box. Outside the cross, larger concentric circles of beds, broken regularly by cross paths, completed the garden design. It was one of the arms of the cross that was sacrificed when the barn was reoriented and the wing added to the house. Today, boxwood-edged beds remain filled with colorful annuals and perennials. Rolled and compacted swept-dirt paths provide a kindly walking surface that is appreciated by older residents of the home.

The central garden path, edged with long beds of roses, still leads to a large and elaborate wooden summer house, a focal terminus to the view down the garden path. Its gothic-inspired windows and latticed walls offer both light and shade to garden strollers. In 1941, John Mead Howells notes in *The Architectural Heritage of the Merrimack* that the "finial spire on the summer house was surmounted by a small scale model of the Old South Church of Newburyport where George Whitefield (1714–1770) preached and where he is buried. The model fell apart some years ago and all trace of it has been lost." Today, there is a simple spire atop the small

building. Through the summerhouse, a set of wooden steps leads down to the second terrace, where the fruit garden was located. Bush fruits, grapes and a few orchard trees grew on this level. The grapes were espaliered on a wooden trellis designed to take advantage of the sunny, south-facing terrace slope. Steps leading down to a third level, where the larger field crops and vegetables were grown and the family horse pastured, are no longer there.

Today, deciduous trees have reclaimed the open fields and pastures of the third terrace. They are quickly encroaching on the fruit garden. However, the pleasure garden is still highly ornamental and colorfully planted. The design, scale and configuration of the existing garden beds have remained unaltered from their original pattern, set out more that 150 years ago.

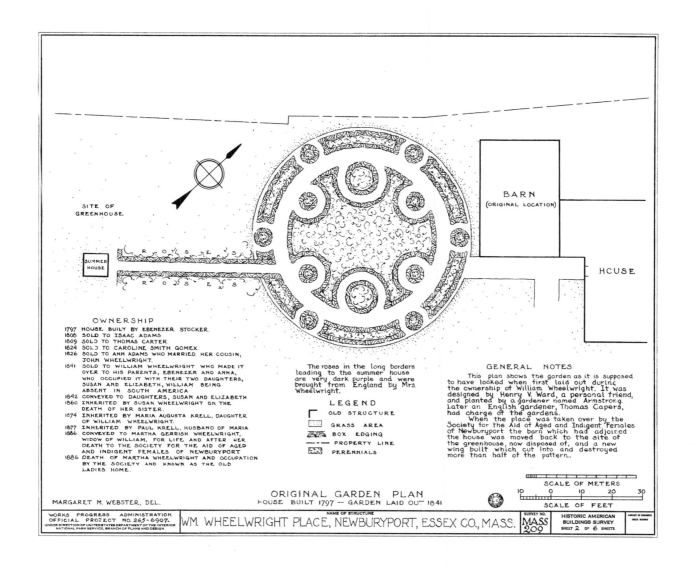

*The pump house originally served both 75 and 73 High Street. (Inset) Detail shows the structure of the ceiling.*

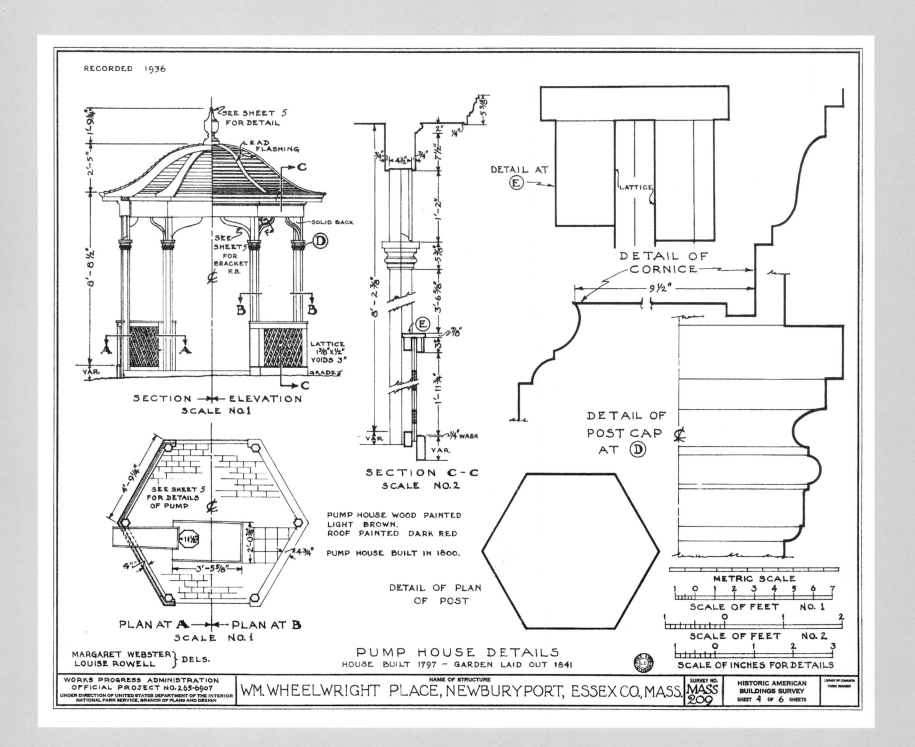

RECORDED 1936

SEE SHEET 5 FOR DETAIL

LEAD FLASHING

SEE SHEET 5 FOR BRACKET F.S.

SOLID BACK

LATTICE 1⅜"x½" VOIDS 3"

VAR.        GRADE

SECTION — ELEVATION
SCALE NO.1

SEE SHEET 5 FOR DETAILS OF PUMP

PLAN AT A — PLAN AT B
SCALE NO.1

MARGARET WEBSTER } DELS.
LOUISE ROWELL

SECTION C-C
SCALE NO.2

¼" WASH
VAR.

PUMP HOUSE WOOD PAINTED LIGHT BROWN.
ROOF PAINTED DARK RED

PUMP HOUSE BUILT IN 1800.

DETAIL OF PLAN
OF POST

DETAIL AT
E

LATTICE

DETAIL OF
CORNICE

9½"

DETAIL OF
POST CAP
AT D

METRIC SCALE
SCALE OF FEET    NO.1
SCALE OF FEET    NO.2
SCALE OF INCHES FOR DETAILS

PUMP HOUSE DETAILS
HOUSE BUILT 1797 — GARDEN LAID OUT 1841

WORKS PROGRESS ADMINISTRATION
OFFICIAL PROJECT NO. 265-6907
UNDER DIRECTION OF UNITED STATES DEPARTMENT OF THE INTERIOR
NATIONAL PARK SERVICE, BRANCH OF PLANS AND DESIGN

NAME OF STRUCTURE
WM. WHEELWRIGHT PLACE, NEWBURYPORT, ESSEX CO., MASS.

SURVEY NO.
MASS
209

HISTORIC AMERICAN
BUILDINGS SURVEY
SHEET 4 OF 6 SHEETS

LIBRARY OF CONGRESS
INDEX NUMBER

### 77 High Street
# WHEELWRIGHT RICHARDSON HOUSE

Abraham Wheelwright, the uncle of William Wheelwright who owned the house at 75 High Street, bought the property adjacent to the recently completed Livermore Lunt Barron Dobson House in 1806, and the large square brick house was built soon afterwards. The handsome front entrance porch, noted for its stylish Corinthian columns, is similar to the porch of the Governor Langdon House in Portsmouth, New Hampshire. Captain John Wills Jr. bought the house in 1825, and his wife and children remained at the property until 1892. The gardens were constructed during their ownership. A successful sea captain and merchant in the East and West Indies, Wills retired from the sea after the War of 1812. He became a banker, joined the Marine Society, and was among the founders of the Salisbury Woolen Mill in 1823. Despite his energetic and varied career, Captain Wills suffered severe business reversals. Upon his death in 1835, there was very little money remaining in his estate and a public auction of the house furnishings was held on the premises. His widow, Sarah, remained in the house until her death in 1875. Only two of their twelve children outlived Sarah, and those heirs remained in the house until 1892.

Under the firm hand of Alice Richardson, whose husband George bought the house in 1908, the garden evolved into one of the most beautiful on High Street. Its Chippendale Gothic garden house, similar to the one still standing in the neighboring yard across Wills Lane, was especially admired by garden visitors. When the house was converted to a nursing home in 1958, the addition of new wings and a parking lot caused the garden to be totally removed. The house, now called Brigham Manor, continues as a nursing and rehabilitation facility.

*(Opposite) Old glass lantern slide. Rear view of the house and garden.*

*Rear view of the house shows position of the small garden pavilion (inset).*

*The large garden area behind 77 High Street is presently completely wooded. The barn at the right is behind the Wheelwright House at 75 High Street.*

By the end of the 18th century, European plantsmen had long been aware of the new plant varieties growing in North America. In Europe, plant collection had been popular for centuries and whole professions had developed around their study, propagation, and care. Early courses in botany were offered in Italy and then, in 1550, at the French University of Montpelier. Soon after, both public and private European botanical gardens were established. Early explorers introduced many new plants to these gardens and to their private patrons. Varieties brought to the old world from the Americas depended on the geographical limits set for the expedition and the purpose of the authorizing agency. Many plant foragers specialized in seeds, or trees and shrubs, others in medicinal plants. Some species, such as marigolds, sunflowers and tobacco plants, were carried to Europe through Spain, others went directly to Paris to join the royal botanic collection in the *Jardin du Roi* in Paris. (Following the French Revolution, the 'garden of the king' was changed to the forthright 'garden of plants,' or *Jardin des Plantes*, which it continues to be called today.) Following North American colonization, England received many seeds and plants from the southern and central Atlantic regions and New England. The pace of this exchange speeded up following the American Revolution, to the benefit of both continents; the old world was interested in developing strains of new plant materials for medicinal and ornamental purposes, while initially those in the new world craved the comfort of the familiar.

Early gardens in Newburyport and other settlements along New England's Atlantic coast took shelter behind board fences, closely hugging the outline of the house for protection and convenience. Both the contour of the gardens and the plants they contained were based on familiar European patterns. Most settlers carried grafts of fruit trees and small pouches of seeds from favorite medicinal plants, herbs, and flowers to the new environment. Trading ships brought English and Dutch seeds and roots to supplement the settlers original horticultural supplies. Like the colonists, this plant material was tough and persist-

ent. Some apple trees planted in the 1620s at the Plymouth plantation were documented as growing into the early twentieth century. By 1630, the garden of Massachusetts Bay Colony Governor John Winthrop was almost Edenesque. His garden on Conant Island in Boston harbor yielded crops that included raspberries, mulberries, currants, and nuts from a variety of species. Gardens were generally small as the ground was hard and rocky and the growing season short. Many of the new arrivals feared or mistrusted the wilderness, ruthlessly destroying the new flora surrounding them and enforcing a clear boundary between the regulated tidiness of civilization and the dark wildness of the unknown; others were fascinated by the unfamiliar and continued the work of the early explorers who had studied the new varieties of trees, shrubs, and flowers and shipped seeds or specimens back to Europe.

As the surrounding wilderness was tamed, its unknown plants and trees became less threatening. Settlers learned to appreciate native fruits, ornamentals, and medicinal plants, slowly incorporating them into their gardens. In Newburyport, summer doorways bloomed with tansy, ox-eye daisies, bouncing Bet, hollyhocks, rosemary, lavender, phlox, heliotrope and larkspur; these were joined in the late 18th century by shrubs, such as the lilac, first brought to England from Persia in the 16th century, and the double-flowered almond, brought to England from Russia in 1683, and then to America before 1750.

As New England towns grew, their shopkeepers received seeds from England and later the Far East to sell on consignment; ladies bonnet shops' were considered especially good locations for selling flower seeds. Newburyport sea captains brought Dutch and English bulbs home from their voyages to sell, swap, or plant, and coastal vessels carried shrubs and trees from New England to the southern states, then returned with southern plants. Gradually, new varieties of garden plants and trees continued to become more available and more desirable.

The early continental and cross-Atlantic exchanges were a precursor of the growing interest triggered on both sides of the ocean by the eighteenth century discoveries of plant-hunter and botanist John

Bartram of Philadelphia, and other similar serious botanists, plant propagators, and hunters. In return for his shipments of new North American plants, Bartram received European varieties for his own garden. This garden evolved into the first botanic collection in America. Bartram sent at least two hundred new plants from the New England forests to English collectors. Dogwoods, fringe trees and lady's-slippers were among familiar favorites sent to Europe; popular trades incorporated into local landscapes included crocus and narcissus bulbs and iris rhizomes. Later, in the 19th century, plant collectors from the Lewis and Clark expedition sent new plants from their western explorations to European and American plantsmen, including the Oregon grape or *Mahonia aquifolium* which is found in many old Newburyport gardens.

By the nineteenth century, North American trees and shrubs became an increasingly important element of European ornamental landscape design. Seeds from American pine, firs, oaks, and cypress became standard offerings of the American and European nursery trade, available to both native and foreign clients. At the same time, many indigenous American plants that had been sent to Europe as oddities were improved by European gardeners and re-introduced to American gardens. Lists of prize winners in horticultural exhibitions hosted by the Newbury-port Horticultural Society mention South American sea rattles, a vine from Havana, a fig tree, Chinese primrose, India plant, smoke tree, and a pomegranate.

Gradually, plant collection and sales became a serious business on both sides of the Atlantic. In the Republic, nursery catalogues developed in the late eighteenth century, first as broadsides and later as booklets. Offerings to customers included both imports and native stock. By the nineteenth century, catalogues offered both seeds and plants, and often divided their material under headings: garden seeds (for the kitchen garden), physical herbs (medicinal use), natives (North American), exotics (not indigenous), greenhouse (needs frost protection), and stove-house (needs heat to thrive). Most included a large choice of fruit trees and berries. Producing a wide variety of fruits throughout the growing season gave orchard owners a fine reputation among other gardeners.

The transport of plants was a difficult problem for nurserymen, plant collectors, and private individuals. Live plants had always suffered at sea from salt spray and the temperature variations of ocean travel. Only a relatively small number survived. Seed was usually shipped coated in beeswax and wrapped in waxed cotton and paper. Plant collectors tried a variety of shipping techniques before the success of the Victorian period glass case. Baskets, wooden frames, and various shaped cabinets had their seasons of popularity. In the mid nineteenth century, the number of surviving plants transported by sea jumped, their survival facilitated by the new glass Wardian cases, invented by Dr. Nathaniel Ward in 1833. These containers created a self-contained micro-climate that raised the percentage of plant survival. The case became the most effective means of carrying plants for long periods and long distances.

The opening of Japan by Commodore Perry in 1854 led to the import of more favorite Newburyport plants: *Magnolia stellata*, hinoki cypress, and Japanese maples. During that century, a wave of unfamiliar exotic Asian plants and trees arrived in America via Europe from India, Japan, and China. Newly introduced rhododendron and azalea species flourished in New England, the Atlantic states, and the South. Plant discoveries by Englishman Robert Fortune and other explorers of the unfamiliar East included lacebark pine, jasmine, and mourning cyprus. It is said that Newburyport's Moulton and Graves gardens, each laid out by an Englishman remembered only as Higgins, incorporated shrubs newly introduced by Fortune.

In 1872, leaders at Boston's Arnold Arboretum began to investigate the feasibility of expeditions to supplement their plant collection. The lofty Arboretum mission was to 'collect, grow and display as far as possible all the trees, shrubs, and herbaceous plants, whether indigenous or exotic, that could be raised in the open in the vicinity of Boston.' Expeditions organized by Charles Sprague Sargent and plant seeker Ernest "Chinese" Wilson introduced more than 500 varieties and ornamentals to gardens local and European. By the end of the nineteenth century, Americans had moved far from their horticultural beginnings. No longer insular, they had become "modern," taking a new and worldly delight in the products of unknown countries and strange cultures.

## 79 High Street
# LIVERMORE LUNT BARRON DOBSON HOUSE

This massive Federal house on the corner of Wills Lane was begun between 1803 and 1805, and was acquired before its completion by Edward St. Loe Livermore, who finished its construction. Livermore added his own touches to the building, including a large second floor ballroom and a first floor bedroom with a private stair to the wine cellar. He was instrumental soon after in establishing the nearby Newburyport Academy at 83–85 High Street. Elected to Congress in 1807, Livermore left his wife in Newburyport to raise their twelve children and took his intellectual eldest daughter Harriet to Washington to serve as his hostess. In 1838, Captain Micajah Lunt acquired the property. Lunt had formed a company to outfit vessels for Pacific coast whaling. One of his ships, the *Merrimack*, arrived back in Newburyport in 1837, carrying over two thousand barrels of whale oil. Perhaps his profits enabled the purchase of the house on High Street. Captain Lunt changed the appearance of the original building by adding elements of the Greek Revival style popular at the time. According to John Mead Howells' *Architectural Heritage of the Merrimack*, "Capt. Lunt removed the old woodwork, the high dadoes and the shutters and put in marble mantles for coal, a new staircase and windows with weights!" Lunt also added the garden.

Howells notes that Lunt's garden was laid out by an Englishman. In a possible confirmation of this, the son of Thomas Bradley, a noted English gardener in the area, remarked that his father had worked on many High Street gardens. Bradley had originally made his reputation in town through his work at Indian Hill, a renowned estate in the neighboring town. It is possible that he designed or served as an advisor on the development of the gardens at this property. A further rumor has it that the same gardener worked on this garden as on the handsome grounds of the estate of Captain Charles M. Bayley at 6 Purchase Street. That garden disappeared long ago.

The pleasure garden behind the house was laid out with box-edged beds, separated by curving walks. As with many other High Street residences, the garden was divided into three terraces, with flights of steps connecting the terraces. A summerhouse on the top terrace formed a terminal focal point, and a small orchard of quince, apple, cherry, and pear grew on the lower terrace. Below, a pump house and watering trough provided water to the animals pastured in the fields.

An article in the 1946 *Boston Sunday Globe* notes that the garden was redesigned in 1878 to include a croquet lawn bordered with heliotrope, peonies, and iris. The summer-

house was used as a shady resting-place during the croquet game. This added croquet area replaced some of the original *parterre* garden beds. Part of the garden was dedicated to roses. Howells mentions many of the old Newburyport favorites found in this garden: prairie, provence, red damask, red button, York and Lancaster, safrano, tea roses, white blush, pink damask, climbing roses, cabbage roses, and "the raspberry rose—a very small rose, white with a pink center having the odor of raspberries."

Today, the original trees have grown tall and wide and the house is barely visible from High Street. The size of the property is much reduced in the back, but the shape of the original lower terracing is apparent in the adjacent yard. The garden is extant, although the garden beds are less defined and cultivated than in the past. The Gothic-inspired lattice summerhouse is one of the nicest in Newburyport and remains a significant feature of the garden. The property is now undergoing restoration.

# Publications

Between 1820 and 1849, the interest in horticultural periodicals produced in America exploded, their numbers jumping from four to approximately thirty, in a reflection of the new interest in gardening. Typical publications of the era included the *American Gardener's Magazine*, Breck's *Book of Flowers*, *Horticultural Register* and *Gardener's Magazine*, as well as publications that focused on a single variety, such as *The Rose: its History, Poetry, Culture, and Classification*. In 1835, The Newburyport Horticultural Society voted that the Society subscribe to the *Horticultural Register* and the *American Gardener's Magazine*. Until the early nineteenth century, horticultural journals and periodicals were produced in England and sent on to subscribers in America. Their numbers increased as cheaper methods of printing and color reproduction brought purchase of the magazines into the price range of the masses. By the mid-19th century, horticulturists found these journals a fine vehicle to spread their theories of style, color, and plant care. The calendar, explaining what chores should be done and when, was the most popular format to convey information. Its directions needed to be adapted to the American climate as it was based on the English seasons. The *Gardener's Calendar for North Carolina and South Carolina* by Robert Squibb was the first book known to discuss only American horticulture. Several other calendars followed the Squibb model, and then in 1806, Bernard M'Mahon published the *American Gardener's Calendar*, the first American book dedicated to general gardening. Calendars and garden almanacs remained the prime format for garden information until 1828. The *American Gardener's Magazine*, founded in 1835, was the first strictly horticultural publication and remained popular for decades. American writing focused on horticultural specialization also began in the early nineteenth century: reflecting the prevalence of orchards, the most popular topic was pomology, the science of fruit cultivation; followed by floriculture, the cultivation of flowers; and later olericulture, the study of plants producing vegetable fats and oils. In England, John Claudius Loudon tirelessly published works on garden history and horticulture; his *Encyclopedia of Gardening* (1822) was the first thorough treatment of the field.

## 83–85 High Street
# OSGOOD BROCKWAY HOUSE

n 1807, this two-story brick house was constructed as the site of the newly established Newburyport Academy, one of the first private schools for boys and girls in the United States. Edward St. Loe Livermore, then living at 79 High Street, was president of the establishing corporation. Perhaps he was motivated by the size of his family; he fathered twelve children. Among the laws and regulations for the Academy's internal government, article six sets the tone of the new establishment:

6. In each department, it shall be an important duty of the instructors, to regulate the temper and conduct of their pupils, and impress their hearts with a sense of religion. To this end, they shall frequently address them on the duties they owe their God, their Savior, their fellow creatures and themselves; on the dangers and temptations incident to their age; and on the advantages and delights of early piety. They shall likewise carefully watch, and endeavor to repress, the first appearances of irregularity and licentiousness.

In 1842, the Academy building was sold to John Osgood and Charles J. Brockway who converted it into a residential duplex. Behind the house, each family built their individual garden, each reflecting the interests of its owner. As with other High Street houses, the property was divided in half, from High Street straight through the center hallway of the house, directly to the rear of the property. This division resulted in two very narrow rear yards with no central axis to the rear door of the dwelling.

Thomas Bradley assisted with the design and plant selection for the Brockway garden, and may have also helped with the Osgood side, although included in John Osgood's sketchbook is a design for his own garden, indicating that he may have laid out his half of the property. An English gardener, Bradley first came to work at Indian Hill, an established estate in West Newbury, and later embarked on a landscape design career in Newburyport.

The Osgood garden, on the west side of the property, included four boxwood-edged *parterres* near the house with a central path terminating in a small, square garden house. The cross paths were entered through a wonderful four-sided clematis-laden arch system. In 1930, the garden was documented by HABS drawings. The sketch reveals that the garden was filled with a profusion of peonies, white roses, larkspur, iris, columbine, box-

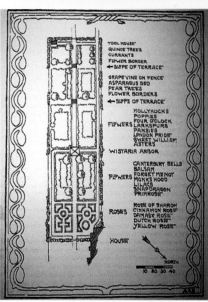

*Garden plan drawn by landscape architect Arthur Shurcliff.*

*1899 photograph by Arthur Shurcliff of boxwood edged parterres in the Brockway garden.*

wood, arborvitae, mock orange, mignonette, heliotrope, sweet alyssum, zinnias, and marigolds. Wisteria, clematis, woodbine and akebia grew up the end of the old barn, at the side of the garden. As with the neighboring Wheelwright House, terraces below the pleasure yard were designed for fruit and vegetable gardens. The Osgood garden was originally separated from the Brockway garden by a spindle and rail fence. After that deteriorated in the 1930s, it was replaced by a band of lilacs, rhododendrons, mock orange, and a strawberry bush. A cross path connected the two gardens in a friendly fashion,

although the two were very different in their layout and their aesthetic aura. The Osgood garden was far simpler.

In 1856, Bradley laid out the Brockway garden on the east side of the property. The plan for this garden was more elaborate than the Osgood garden, with a long central path flanked by geometric garden parterres on the upper level. A latticed summerhouse sat at the end of the central garden path. Through the summerhouse, a set of stairs led down to another, smaller cut-flower garden, beyond which lay additional terraces filled with fruits and vegetables.

In 1899, a young Arthur Shurcliff visited the Brockway garden and documented its styling and contents for *New England Monthly Magazine*, writing:

The garden is in a remarkable state of preservation. It lies near the house, upon a gently sloping hillside, and it is broken by terraces, which are mounted by short flights of steps. It is surrounded by a high close fence, heavily clothed in vines, and no one could imagine from without that such a garden existed; it is as much removed from the street and its traffic as a room in the house itself. Old-fashioned flowers of all kinds flourish in it.... An arbor makes a pleasant resting-place even at high noon. There is evidence that the garden is regarded by the household as a part of the establishment necessary to their daily life, and there is no suggestion that it is a place for display or that it is a fanciful ornament.

As for the design of the garden, Shurcliff notes:

Although the old designers of gardens realized the value of formality in design and its direct relation to the rectangular lines of the house plan, yet they seem to have thought it unnecessary to center their gardens upon a particular window or door of the house. They placed them where convenience dictated, and considerations of economy in the uses of their land often prevented an axial relation of house and garden.

Considerations of *ownership* in the use of the land often prevented an axial relationship of house and garden in the shared houses of High Street. The back door of houses designed as duplexes shared that common space while the two side doors become the main door for each half-house.

Shurcliff's plan documented the contents of the garden, similar to those growing at the Osgood half of the house: "Periwinkle, gaillardia, hibiscus, honeysuckle, clematis, rudbeckia, roses, iris, gladiolus, foxglove, poppies, peonies, Canterbury bells, bee-balm, sweet William, mignonette, bloodroot, lemon and tiger lilies, phlox, deutzia, monkshood, snapdragons, bachelor buttons, campanula, dahlias, sunflowers, morning glories and rhododendrons."

Shurcliff's unpublished journal made further observations about the garden:

A few of the more common flowers cultivated are mentioned in the accompanying plan. It is worthy of notice that few of the modern and extravagant double forms are to be found among them. The rose garden is pretty in design, and as it is in the most elaborate portion of the garden, it is fittingly placed near the house. The walks that separate the beds are bordered with neat box edgings. This garden may fairly be called a type of the old-fashioned garden. The long narrow plan, the central walk, the terraces, the presence of flowering fruit trees in the flower borders, the arbor, and the seclusion of high border screens are to be found in nearly every example.

Though this is one of the first High Street gardens to be documented in any formal way; it has not survived as well as many others. The garden remained intact into the 1930s, however; it has not survived into the twenty-first century. The property changed hands many times in the last century, and after World War II, the state of the garden deteriorated. Today, only significant trees, outbuilding foundations, and a few of the plantings remain.

## 89–91 High Street
# THE MOULTON HOUSE

The Moulton property is unique among the historic homes along Newburyport's High Street as it has remained in the same extended family since 1809. The land was originally purchased by Joseph Moulton from his neighbor Ebenezer Greenleaf for $450. The Moulton name was already recognized in New England for silver-smithing, and examples of William and Joseph Moulton's skill are found today in both private collections and in the decorative arts department of major American museums. Currier's *History of Newburyport* mentions William Moulton, goldsmith and jeweller, who carried on the manufacture of teaspoons, porringers, tablespoons and thimbles. Construction of the double house seen on High Street today was completed in 1809 by Joseph Moulton and his son. In 1840, Joseph hired a man to lay out the garden. Family records mention that this work was done by "an English gardener named Clifford" who had recently come to Newbury. He may also have designed and planted other Newburyport gardens. The present generation continues a nearly two-century tradition of family stewardship of this High Street property, caring for both the Federal home and the old garden.

The Moulton house sits a short distance from the street on a small but steeply terraced hill. From 1809 until today, its two side entrances have served as the main entrance for each half of the divided house. Brick paths connect these side entrances to High Street. The front entrance is never used and serves more as the symbolic line of division for the house and property.

According to the original plan, the upper pleasure terrace behind the house was divided into two halves. A large wooden barn and grape arbor occupied the western half of the terrace; a small lane connected this area to the street. According to the Historic American Buildings Survey (HABS) plan, the barn was taken down in 1910 and replaced by a lawn and perennial gardens. An elaborate boxwood-edged garden, set out in a double hourglass design, occupied the eastern half of the terrace. This garden was designed by the gardener Clifford. Beyond the barn lay the family orchard; beyond the *parterre* garden a straight path bisected the berry garden and led to the summerhouse. An herb and wild garden were of special interest. The summerhouse, which was later moved to the southeast corner of the *parterre* garden, was designed in the gothic style with narrow lattice panels support-ing the sweeping curve of the lattice roof. Dutchman's pipe, a vine with wide elephant-ear shaped leaves and curious pipe-like brown flowers, covered the structure. Inside, a round seat was built into each corner and it still houses an ancient pew from Newburyport's old

*(Opposite) The latticed summerhouse on the Moulton property has been the backdrop for many family occasions. (Top) Silversmith Joseph Moulton observes his garden in 1900. (Bottom) Current owners Dr. Marc Cendron and Jennifer Day on their wedding day in 1984.*

South Church. An acorn is carved into the coping. Four Chinese red turrets decorate the corners of the summerhouse roof, a nod to the Chinese influence that affected New England gardens and garden furniture during the early nineteenth century, reflecting the increased trading links with the east.

The north end of the garden was framed by a high lattice fence and arched entry. This fence separated the drying yard and brick service yard immediately behind the house from the view of those strolling in the garden. Another wooden arch served as a focal point at the end of the *parterre* garden. Wooden grape arbors added another architectural element to an otherwise service-oriented side yard.

The *parterre* garden was designed in a double hourglass pattern with two circular garden beds and a third elliptical bed. All the beds were edged with boxwood, as were the straight paths framing the garden on four sides. In the center of the elliptical bed was a Catawba rhododendron, said to be the oldest plant in the garden, pre-dating the 1840 design. Mountain laurel, roses and sweetshrub dominated the rest of this bed. Roses included damask, moss, scotch, prairie and

*This photograph appeared in* The Mentor *magazine in June 1916. (Inset) Family members in the garden with their dog.*

the appealing Baltimore Belle, with its masses of white buds tipped with pink. Perennials were featured in the two circular beds and filled the remainder of the garden. Beginning with the early snowdrops and continuing through the Christmas roses (Hellebores), some plant variety in the garden was always in bloom.

The grape arbor supported Rogers or Salem Blood grapes, as well as Isabella, Niagara and Delaware varieties. Planted in 1840, the vine still produces fruit, and reputedly is the source for the "best grape jelly." The orchard featured apples, and later pear trees. Pears became popular in Newburyport later in the nineteenth century. Quince, currant, smokebush, spirea, mock orange and other flowering shrubs edged the property and ensured privacy. The Oregon grape, *Mahonia nervosa*, was started as a cutting from the Cushing garden across High Street. The Cushing original was reputedly brought from the English garden of popular nineteenth century author Sir Walter Scott.

89 High Street was inherited by Elizabeth Little Whiting, the grandmother of the present owner. She was a cousin of Elizabeth Coleman (Little) Moulton, the last Moulton descendant to live in that side of the house. In 1927, the American Horticultural Society asked Elizabeth Coleman Moulton to write an article about the garden. At that time the garden was in excellent condition. By 1942, during World War II, the garden, like many others along High Street, was in a downward cycle of disrepair. Elizabeth Whiting's mother-in-law, Bertha Whiting from Auburn, Maine, restored the garden to a new period of great beauty.

Mrs. Whiting made the garden's reclamation her life work. She began by uncovering beds so overgrown by tangles of roses and brush that it was impossible to tell what lay smothered beneath. Bit by bit, uncovering and defining paths, box hedges, and plants, she brought the garden to life. In an interview in the July 1955 edition of *The Home Garden* magazine, Mrs. Whiting, then 71, explained, "One side of our garden looked dead. But after we worked and worked on it, we found a definite path under the tangle. On the fence side of the path, we discovered a profusion of wild flowers. Now we have European barberry, lilacs, honeysuckle, spirea, snowberry, and two varieties of forsythia." To reestablish the garden borders once again, a major piece of the restoration process became propagation of new boxwood from the old—and this tradition continues today. Mrs. Whiting proudly

*In this later photograph, the boxwood edging has matured.*

commented on the success of her box restoration: "We had a visitor from Virginia a few summers ago—one of the men connected with the Williamsburg restoration project. He told me our boxwood compares more than favorably with the boxwood in the restored Colonial gardens there. He was particularly impressed with the beauty of the design." Following her death, the garden slowly declined again as family situations shifted and interest in the garden waned.

The present owners, Doctor Marc Cendron and his wife Jennifer Day, presently share the divided property with Marc's mother, Norrine (Whiting) Cendron. The couple, who was married in front of the summerhouse, is gradually re-awakening the original spirit of the nineteenth century garden. Despite the demands of work and a young family, the garden is again in a cycle of restoration. Following the death of Bertha Whiting, her daughter-in-law, Elizabeth Whiting, mother of Norrine (Whiting) Cendron, replicated the design in a hand-drawn sketch. This sketch guides the present restoration. Two of the boxwood circles within the large well-established box rectangle are complete; the third bed of the double hourglass was completed in the fall of 2003.

As it has traditionally, the lure of the old garden continues to play an ongoing role in the life of the extended Moulton family members who are currently serving as its caretakers.

(Inset) Bertha Whiting reclaimed the garden in the middle of the twentieth century.

*The summerhouse at the end of the grape arbor no longer remains but is reproduced in the garden next door at 87 High Street. The lattice summerhouse seen in earlier photographs is on the left side of the photograph.*

## 98 High Street
# THE CUSHING HOUSE

Open the creaking iron gate and stroll the short distance to the front door of the Cushing house and you have already crossed the threshold of time. This small front yard, now ornamented with grass and brick, was laid out by William and Sarah Hunt when they built their brick Federal house and two-story wooden barn in 1808. They would hardly recognize the property today because it is both larger and more decorative than their early nineteenth century holding.

Sarah was left to raise her children in their High Street home after her husband's death in 1818. To ease family finances, she sold the western half of the house and the barn to John Cushing, and kept the eastern half for her family. The large brick house occupied most of the 2/10-acre lot, and dirt lanes connected the barn behind the house to High Street and Fruit Street, leaving only small strips of land along the lanes for planting a few apple and pear trees.

Sarah sold her half of the house to John Cushing in 1822, and the house and lot were reunited into a single family home. Between 1822 and 1849, John expanded his property to ¼ acre, and may have planted more fruit trees, because in 1829 the family gathered enough apples and pears to sell the surplus in downtown shops. The Cushings raised their six children here until John's death in 1849.

William and John, Jr. inherited the property from their father and again divided the house into two halves. Their mother, Elizabeth Cushing, lived in the eastern half of the house until her death in 1865, and John, Jr., along with his wife, and five children occupied the western half. William and his family lived nearby at 18 Fruit Street and their step-brother Caleb Cushing lived across the street at 63 High. The corner bustled with activity as the town, and the Cushing family, continued to grow.

After William sold his ownership in the property to his brother in 1867, John seized the opportunity to expand and improve the grounds. He bought the house and land next door on Fruit Street, picked up his barn and turned it to face Fruit Street, kept land enough for a new lane to the barn, and sold the now smaller neighboring house lot to Jane Brown.

With the enlarged property and the extra room afforded by the relocated barn, John began an extensive gardening campaign. He bought twenty-seven varieties of roses in 1877, set out new boxwood in 1894, planted grass in 1895, and purchased "large plants" in 1897. He hired help to "make the garden," and to repair or rebuild his fences. He, in fact, transformed the

*Miss Margaret Cushing lived in this brick Federal family home throughout her 100-year life span. Since her death in 1955, the house has been the home of the Historical Society of Old Newbury.*

property into what we recognize today. Narrow paths wound through the garden, geometric beds were filled with roses, larkspur, phlox, iris, and gilly flowers. Fruit trees shaded panels of green grass and the colorful garden beds. Behind the barn, the vegetable garden was planted with sweet corn, beans, and other family favorites. Dahlias, marigolds, alyssum, snapdragons, daffodils and crocus bloomed in seasonal splendor. In 1905, an arbor seat was brought from another family garden to visually link the lower portion of the garden behind the barn with the summerhouse at the head of the garden.

Margaret and her brother Lawrence took care of the property after their father's death in 1906. The summerhouse was renovated by William Graves Perry, a High Street neighbor. Perry and his partners later became the architects responsible for the restoration of Colonial Williamsburg. An unofficial steward of her family's legacy, Margaret recorded her memories of the house and the garden through the Historic American Buildings Survey and wrote about her memories for small local clubs where she held membership. In 1955, when she died at the age of one hundred, the Historical Society of Old Newbury acquired the house and grounds. In Newburyport, Miss Cushing's memory is treasured for her New England restraint. Rather than installing a bathroom, Miss Cushing would place her towel over her arm and stroll down High Street to her neighbor and cousin Miss Todd's house, where she would enjoy a once-a-week bath.

The garden aged with its occupants, and the geometric bed designs and paths had all but disappeared by 1965 when the garden was revitalized by garden consultant Isadore Smith and Historical Society members Nancy and Benjamin Stone. In 1995, another revitalization campaign for the garden was begun with the hope that the gardens could be restored to their earlier splendor when they were designed and tended by John Cushing, Jr. Guided by garden historian and designer Lucinda Brockway, who made an extensive study of the history of both the house and the garden, a modified design based on the archival documentation for the garden design was created that would enable volunteers to care for the simplified garden while ensuring the authenticity of plant material and the nineteenth century spirit of the overall design.

John and his two children, Margaret and Lawrence, lived in the Cushing family home for their entire lives. Their keen interest in the property, in their family's Newburyport legacy, and in the continued preservation of the house and grounds, has guided the Historical Society of Old Newbury in its continued operation. Today, we can open the gate, wander the garden, and step into the past—a history rich in the sights, smells, and sounds of Newburyport and its environs since 1808.

This peach tree is no longer in the Cushing House garden but the memo below does show the importance placed on fruit hybridization, and the unique varieties found in Newburyport gardens.

Memo: re Peach Tree
To: Mr. Woodwell
From: Mr. Goodhue

The peach tree in the garden was purchased by Miss Cushing's father from some one in New York State under an agreement with the seller that the peach stones should not be planted but should be destroyed; the idea apparently being that the tree was unique in the United States.

The peaches grown on the tree were small and of a mouse color. The inside of the skin was a dark red. When preserved the skinless peach was an extremely dark red.

Miss Cushing asked one or two horticulturists about the tree but was never able to find out its kind or where it originally came from.

*This memo was sent from Laurence C. Goodhue, a cousin of Miss Margaret Cushing, to Roland H. Woodwell, a New England historian, in approximately 1948. The memo was found in a collection of Newburyport family papers.*

*The original summerhouse had an open lattice roof. The current house was redesigned by the firm of Perry, Shaw & Hepburn, Architects, Boston, MA in 1934, based on an old photograph of the original.*

# Roses in Miss Margaret Cushing's Garden at 98 High Street

*Rosa alba,* small double.
Known to have been in the family at least as early as 1776.

*Rosa alba,* small semi-double.
Rosa alba has been found in Piedmont, Denmark, France and Saxony. It can be traced through centuries of European civilization with more certainty than any other rose. Was introduced to English gardens before 1597. There are many varieties—single white, semi-double, large and small double, and some ranging from pale flesh to a clear light pink, the latter known as Maiden's Blush.

Maiden's Blush

Red Moss Rose
Moss roses are variations from the old cabbage rose and have been known as far back as 1596. They have been officially reported in France in 1696 and in Italy in 1735, but never became popular until the nineteenth century. The original was a large pink variety, heavily mossed, which is still to be had.

*Rosa centifolia,* Old Cabbage rose.
Pliny and Theophrastus mentioned what seems to have been this rose on Mt. Panga, and Herodotus mentions it in Macedonia near the ancient garden of Midas. It was introduced to England by the Crusaders, and again in the sixteenth century by the Walloons. The wild type has never been found. It is one of the parents of the modern Hybrid Perpetuals and Hybrid Teas.

York and Lancaster
The true rose of this name is a Damask rose, and is first mentioned by Monardes in 1551, more than half a century after the wars it commemorates. It is often confused with the more common *Rosa Mundi,* which is a variety of *Rosa gallica,* striped red and white. York and Lancaster is more usually not striped, but has some petals white, some red or pink.

Seven Sisters Rose
A variety of the Japanese rose brought from China in 1815, through members of the East India Company, to England.

General Jacqueminot
Produced by Roussel, in France, 1852. It is the most famous red rose in existence and one of the parents from which nearly all the modern red roses have been produced.

Thausendshon
Produced by a German nursery in 1906. It became immediately popular, and went round the world in less than 25 years after it originated. It is still one of the most beautiful climbers.

*This list, compiled on June 29, 1937, was found in a collection of Newburyport family papers.*

*The early cobblestone yard still exists. The path in the right hand photograph leads to an arch that originally stood in the garden at 90 High Street, where it framed a ship's figurehead. The figurehead is now restored and is on display at the Historical Society of Old Newbury.*

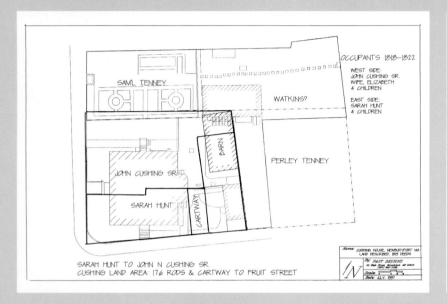

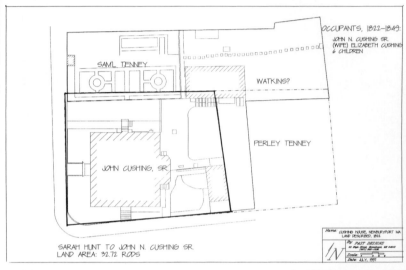

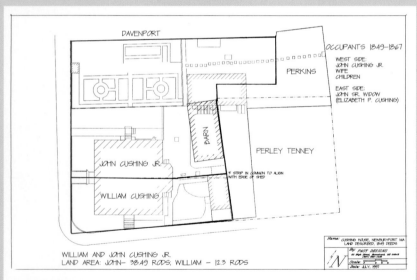

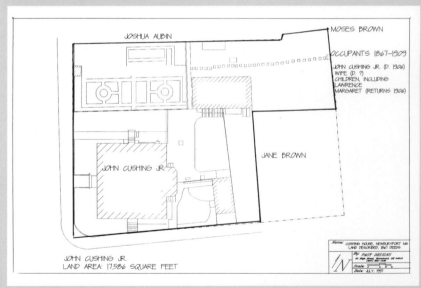

Four plans showing the evolution of the Cushing House property. Plan opposite shows the current configuration of the property based on the garden layout as it was from 1867–1905, according to research done by Lucinda Brockway. This plan was implemented in 1998.

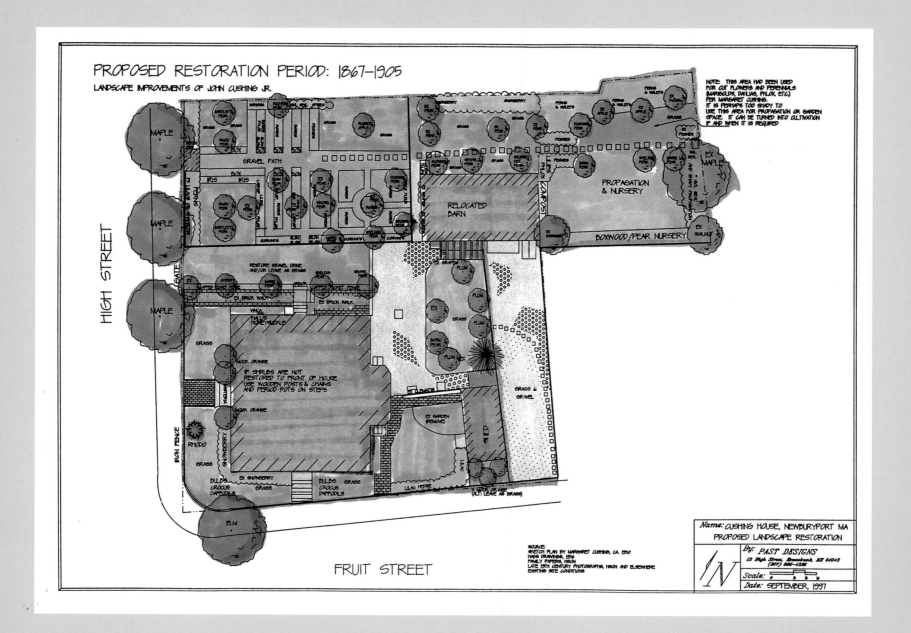

## 190 High Street
# MOSS LEARNED NELSON HOUSE

The recorded history of this beautifully preserved High Street property begins in 1695, when Tezrah Bartlett inherited the land from her father. Tezrah Bartlett was married to Hathorn Coker, a Quaker, and in 1768 their heirs set aside "three rods" of the property as a "Friends" burying ground. This burying ground was located on what is now the third level of the garden, beyond what was formerly the vegetable garden. Nothing but memories remain of the burying ground today, as the graves were moved in the previous century. In 1803, the Reverend James Moss, the rector of Newburyport's St. Paul's church, lived in the present house; upon his death in the 1840s the land again passed to a daughter, who is believed to have laid out the original garden.

The garden owes its longevity to Henry Learned, who rented the property in 1916 and purchased it in 1921. His extensive work included the thorough rejuvenation of the garden *parterres*, and much of what remains in the garden today is the result of his effort and interests. His daughter Lorna inherited the house and eventually simplified the garden design, removing some of the more complicated terrace patterns but retaining the overall design and planting style.

The layout of the garden is believed to remain from the 1840s. The more formal flowerbeds were located close to the house with a kitchen garden and fruit garden to the rear, at the lowest level. Located on the northern side of High Street, this property did not have the dramatic topography of its neighbors across the street, but instead was built on a gradually declining slope which fell gently away from the house northward toward the Merrimack River and downtown Newburyport.

The garden was separated into three areas by a series of tall hedges. A long central path connected the garden spaces and served as the spine to the garden which was constructed on a central axis with the sitting terrace behind the house. Boxwood hedges lined both sides of the central path, edging the wide perennial borders behind them. On each side of the first level of the garden were circular box-lined beds that were replaced by lawn when Miss Learned took over the care of the garden. This change was an attempt to simplify the daunting amount of maintenance required to care for the extensive property. An early twentieth century rose arbor sits over the central path at the end of the first level of the garden. Its benches are an inviting draw to wander down the main path to a sheltered resting place at the garden's far end. The arbor attractively frames that view. According to clippings found in the Newburyport Garden Club archives, the garden was famous dur-

*(Top) Lorna Learned seen here in 1993, had a life-long commitment to her garden.*

ing the 1930s for its Knight's Spears, similar to plants blooming in England's historic Hampton Court, Fraxinella or gas plant, a Flaming Fame bush, and a silk tree. Today the house has again changed hands. The rear garden level has been simplified for the use of a young family with children. The remaining nineteenth century garden stands as a testament to the many generations that have taken their turn in shaping and tending the garden beds, ensuring the survival of both the garden and its engaging history of female inheritance. The longtime Learned gardeners, first John Mullarkey, then John Savukinas, and Newburyport landscape designer Lillian Newbert, working both with Lorna Learned and current owners Jenny and Ted Nelson, deserve recognition for their contribution to the garden's continuance.

*The long perennial border at the center of the yard changes levels at the arbor. (Opposite) The wisteria covered central door facing High Street.*

*Detail of Miss Learned's renowned gas plant showing both white and pink varieties.*

*Photograph taken during Henry Learned's ownership of the property. Peggy Connolly and Ruth Connolly Burke stroll through the garden in 1947.*

## 201 High Street
# JACKSON DEXTER KELLEY QUILL HOUSE

This handsome property was one of the few along High Street in the early nineteenth century that did not display the geometric French style garden. The house rose to prominence in the late eighteenth century during the ownership of the shrewd, self-promoting "Lord" Timothy Dexter, one of the most famous and infamous characters in Newburyport history. It fell into disrepair following his death, then was revitalized after 1853 in the picturesque style of the Victorian era and eventually became a Massachusetts horticultural landmark.

The house was designed and built in 1771 by Jonathan Jackson, one of the most successful early Newburyport merchants. He immediately planted trees and gardens. Jackson brought three wives to this house, one the sister of his next door neighbor and dear friend John Tracy, but in 1795 he was forced to sell it after being unable to resolve severe personal financial reverses. A sea captain bought the property. His estate sold it to Newburyport oddity Timothy Dexter. Dexter biographer Samuel Knapp provides an early description of his purchase: "It was a princely chateau, standing on the height of land about a quarter of a mile from the river. The grounds had been laid out by intelligent artists from England and France. A lovelier spot, or a more airy mansion, Lucullus could not have wished for." Dexter, a remarkable entrepreneur, married into a fortune, added to it, and ultimately lost it at the end of his life by indulging his whims on the High Street estate. When Dexter advertised his property for sale, he mentioned the extensive garden, but it was the variety of wooden statues displayed on fifteen foot pedestals around the front yard that was most notable during his ownership. In his philosophical publication, *A Pickle for the Knowing Ones*, Dexter described more than fifty of the statues that decorated his door yard. Most were larger than life-size, and each had an identifying plaque at the base. Fashioned by local ship carpenter Joseph Wilson who had honed his skills on ship figureheads, they included presidents Washington, Jefferson, and Adams, Benjamin Franklin, an Indian chief, a travelling preacher, two grenadiers, two lions, one lamb, and two statues of Dexter, one with a plaque that read: "I am the first in the East, the first in the West and the greatest philosopher in the Western world." Appropriately, his garden held statues of Adam and Eve. A summerhouse was also in the garden. It was well known throughout Newburyport, as Dexter kept his tomb in its basement. The garden was the location of Dexter's famous mock funeral, conducted as a dress rehearsal while he was still alive. Following that ceremony, the story goes that he raged at his wife, incensed that her funeral tears were not sufficiently convincing. Save for the presidents, the statues supposedly were knocked from their bases during a

*(Opposite) Silk screened poster of house cupola done in the 1980s by Robert Preston. (Above) Photgraphs taken during the ownership of George Corliss. Rear view of house and barn.*

When my father came to Newburyport he was employed by Capt. Thomas Warren Goodwin who then operated a commercial greenhouse in the rear of his residence on Prospect Street. He lived in a large square house with an observation platform on its roof. One late-May day in 1890 he summoned my father to the roof and bade him look about. It was a beautiful day and from that vantage-point the city was a veritable sea of blossoms. Lilacs, pear trees and horse chestnuts made a pleasing contrast with the blue of the sky and harbor: after a while Capt. Goodwin said, "Never let anyone tell you that the Garden of Paradise was in some foreign place. It's here before our eyes."

Old Fashioned Gardens,
*unpublished paper by Frank J. McGregor, July 23, 1941,*
*Archives: Historical Society of Old Newbury*

violent September gale in 1815 following Dexter's death, and were later sold at auction: The most money ($5) was paid for the Goddess of Fame; the traveling preacher sold for 50 cents.

Dexter died impoverished and the house and grounds deteriorated badly. At times the house sat empty; during one period it was used as a tavern. By the mid-1800s all that was left of the garden was a row of fine apple trees probably planted by Jackson. In 1853, Dr. Elbridge G. Kelley purchased the property and named his new home "The Evergreens." Kelley was a politician as well as a gardener. Serving as Newburyport's mayor in 1871, he greeted President Ulysses S. Grant when the presidential train passed through the town on its way to Maine as the local band played 'Hail to the Chief.' The mayor was a knowledgeable plantsman who transformed what was left of the Dexter property to a horticultural showplace, repairing the house and revitalizing the grounds with trees and shrubs in a clipped and highly groomed interpretation of landscape designer Andrew Jackson Downing's picturesque style.

Kelley set out hundreds of trees and shrubs. He was recognized for the many varieties of pear in his orchard as well as for his other fruit trees. Most amazing was the diversity of ornamentals, both native and imported. He planted sugar, red, silver, striped Norway, purple, Negundo and English maples; purple, English, broadleaf, weeping and American elms; American, English, purple, copper, and silver beeches; plus American larch, Florida cyprus, and varieties of magnolias and hawthornes. To that, Kelley added tulip, coffee, judas, koelruteria, catalpa, paulonia, and gum trees. Hedges of hemlock, barberry and arborvitae lined the walks that interconnected the ponds, meadows and gardens. Nearly one hundred varieties of roses, interspersed with perennials and annuals produced color throughout the season. Later, Kelly built extensive greenhouses and filled them with fruit trees and exotic plants that bloomed throughout the winter. Clipped and manicured to perfection, Kelley's masterpiece surpassed High Street's earlier Federal gardens in scale, composition, and contents.

Emily and George Corliss, who had invented a successful steam engine, owned the extraordinary property from 1874–1897. Following his death, Mrs. Corliss memorialized her husband's interest in the Young Men's Christian Association (YMCA) movement with the construction of a massive stone YMCA building in downtown Newburyport on the corner of State Street and Harris. It burned in 1977. Madame Katherine Westcott Tingley, a eurhythmic

*This open yard is now Dexter Lane and is lined with many houses.*

dancer, teacher, practitioner and leader of the Theosophy Society bought the house in 1909, remaining there until the sect moved its headquarters to California. George Learned, whose brother lived at 190 High Street, was the next owner. His widow remained in the house until the early 1960s.

Following World War II, the extended property was subdivided. Its original terraces can still be seen in the topography at the rear of the house. The greenhouse was dismantled and today the barn is a separate residence. The house has suffered fires and undergone restoration. Now reduced to a residential size corner lot, the massive residence and its surrounding fence retain their commanding, heavily handsome Georgian aura. Save for the old trees in the front yard, the horticultural wonders of the old property have all but vanished, preserved only in a large cache of black and white photographs.

(Opposite) These views of the property are now completely changed as the land has been developed. The pond has been filled and most of the trees have been removed.

# Growing Plants Under Glass

Home vegetable gardens provided staples for the family table in the 18th, 19th, and even the early 20th centuries. The terraced back yards of High Street, facing the afternoon sun, were ideal for growing vegetables or annual ornamentals. The New England growing season was extended by the use of sun-warmed cold frames and hot beds that sheltered seedling vegetables and flowers from the late killing frosts common to New England springs. Easily built cold frames—unheated, partially buried box-like structures with glass tops—protected seedlings from Newburyport's chill east winds. Hot beds were similar but more complex; animal manure, steam, hot air, or water heated the planting soil from below. Like the larger and more sophisticated above ground glass house or green house, the cold frame and hot bed could be rudimentarily adjusted for heat and cold.

The European *orangerie*, the south-facing building designed to winter over lemon, orange, bay, and other tender trees, was the forerunner of the heated glasshouse. In 18th century America, even minimally heated glass houses were unusual and available only to the wealthy; most gardeners had to be content with the traditional means of heating:

sunny windows. By the mid-19th century, large scale gardening under glass was made possible by a series of scientific breakthroughs—primarily by the inventions of frost resistant, waterproof cast iron and plate glass, as well as by the new availability of efficient circulating systems for dependable heating. British inventor J.C. Loudon perfected the use of a malleable wrought iron glazing bar, which could be bent and curved to serve as the frame in large domed all-glass plant houses. Among the larger and more ambitious ones built in America was the elegant 1879 palm house constructed in San Francisco's Golden Gate Park. By the latter years of the century, prefabricated parts for glass houses and conservatories were advertised in gardening journals and building supply catalogues. With this breakthrough, it became possible for the amateur gardener in cold climates to protect and grow tender and exotic plant materials throughout the winter. These separate glass houses and glass additions were popular in Newburyport among homeowners such as Dr. Elbridge Kelley and George Corliss in the Dexter House, and in the homes of other renowned Newburyport plantsmen such as Captain Charles Bayley and William Ashby.

*Glass house at the rear of 201 High Street.*

Now a word or two about the things which grew in our old gardens. It would seem a simple task to take an old catalogue or two and compile a list of the available plants of the period. Actually, while this would be a help, it would by no means result in a comprehensive list because this seafaring populace was inquisitive and acquisitive mortals who brought uncounted things from foreign lands for their gardens, often long before they were officially known to the catalogue makers. Captain Atkinson, of the United Fruit Company kept a reward for new and rare orchids posted with all the company's ships and agents. At the turn of the twentieth century he continued to accumulate more than his small hothouse could contain. When a new lot arrived he would call my father and together they would have to decide which of the older plants to discard in order to make room for the newcomers.

Old Fashioned Gardens,
*unpublished paper by Frank J. McGregor—July 23, 1941,*
*Archives: Historical Society of Old Newbury*

## Mount Rural
# NEWBURYPORT HIGH SCHOOL

Mount Rural was one of the last agricultural properties to survive the pressures of urbanization on High Street in the first half of the twentieth century. The land on the corner of what was then County Road and the "road to the swamp" was originally granted to Archelaus Woodman in the 17th century, and it remained in his family for several generations. Houses on the property were built, added to, and replaced as families moved in and then moved on. By 1820 the property was basically a large gentleman's farm built by Dr. Isaac Smith. The massive main structure sat on the hill a short distance back from the road, surrounded by open fields, scattered trees, and outbuildings.

The simple garden behind the house was a square plot enclosed by a fence. Two straight paths divided it into four smaller squares further sub-divided *parterre* fashion. The easterly plot was for annuals, the southerly for perennials, the westerly for flowering shrubs, and in the summer the northerly plot was filled with tender shrubs. Oleander, hibiscus, gardenia, acuba, camellias, and lemon-verbena were planted in pots or tubs and used as decorative focal points in the northerly square, then carried into the house before frost. A latticed summerhouse stood at the southerly end of the central path. Its front was flush with the fence, while the structure itself stood in the hayfield. At some point, an enclosed deer park was at the front of the property.

Captain Joshua Hale and his daughter Alice L. Atkinson owned the property before its destruction. The stone walls and landscaped lawns of the once elegant Mount Rural estate were retained in the twentieth century, when the house was razed and the property subdivided into one large lot for the new High School and smaller lots for houses. The original large central block of the first High School building is now incorporated into the expanded school structure. It was designed by Newburyport architect Edwin Dodge.

*(Opposite) Rear of the house that once stood on Mt. Rural.*
*(Above) Newburyport High School built circa 1937 and renovated in 2002.*

*Corner of Toppan's Lane and High Street shown in a 1935 photograph before the houses on Mt. Rural were torn down. (Inset) Looking toward the corner of Toppan's Lane and High Street. The High Street houses remain today.*

*July 21, 1891, a fundraising balloon event was held on Mount Rural to benefit the Griffin Home for Aged Men. During the Civil War, the same Allen family balloonists entertaining Newburyporters had surveyed the countryside behind the Confederate lines, providing early aerial reconnaissance for the Union army.*

## 281 High Street
# MILTMORE HUSK HEERSINK HOUSE

Although the primary garden at the Miltmore Husk Heersink house in the northwesterly end of Newburyport was not built until nearly one hundred years after the nineteenth century historic High Street gardens, it is a noteworthy garden space as it reflects the national surge toward Colonial Revival design during the 1920s.

In 1809, when the house was initially built as a parsonage for the Reverend James Miltmore, minister of the Belleville Congregational Church on the opposite side of High Street, the grounds were minimally landscaped and remained so until the early twentieth century. The initial improvement made to the property was the Miltmore family purchase of the lot adjacent to their home. They constructed a house near the street on this property, which they subsequently subdivided and sold. The Miltmores retained the bulk of the land behind the second house as part of their own property, giving them an unusually wide backyard which was very different from the narrow elongated yards of properties closer to town. After the death of the pastor, his son, Captain Andrew Miltmore, owner and captain of the ship "Jane," remained in the house until his death. Immediately, another Belleville Church minister, Reverend Daniel T. Fiske, bought the house as a gift for his daughter. The Husk family purchased the house in the 1920s. Mr. Husk was the inventor of a popular shoe last, and the creator of the Huskee Peach.

Initially, the garden had a central path that ran from the gate to the top of the hill at the back of the property. The hill was crowned with an unusual latticed summerhouse; unusual, as there was an outside flight of stairs leading to a rooftop observation platform. At that time it was possible to see the river from the hilltop as the houses and trees that are presently across the street were not yet there. In the 1850s, a *parterred* shrubbery was planted on the left of the hill, and another shrubbery bed was placed in front of the barn. A horse-chestnut tree whose lower branches grew out horizontally for about three feet, then turned at right angles and shot straight up stood on the edge of the street. This odd pattern of growth was due to the Reverend Miltmore, who had bent and tied the young branches as a moral lesson to his Sunday-school classes. The minister hoped to impress upon them the importance of youthful training, and to emphasize the old saying, "As the twig is bent, so grows the tree." This tree was directly in the way of Harry M. Husk's planned driveway entrance and was removed when the Husk family purchased the property.

*The Belleville Church where the Reverend James Miltmore preached is seen across the tree tops, on the other side of High Street.*

Mrs. Husk was fascinated by horticulture, and soon created an extensive flower garden in the broad sweep of the spacious rear yard. Clearly inspired by the older High Street gardens and by the contemporary Colonial Revival movement, the garden was designed with axial and cross-axial paths lined with boxwood and punctuated by summerhouses set at pathway intersections. Shaded garden arbors were a vantage point for viewing the rose and woodland gardens as well as flower beds filled with colorful perennials and annuals.

Although on a much grander scale than Newburyport's long-established nineteenth century gardens, this property reflected many of their basic design ideals and was an excellent example of the Colonial Revival interpretation of the principles of American landscape design. In its prime, the Husk garden was one of the most celebrated twentieth century High Street gardens. This complex undertaking was not a garden for a single person to care for; Mrs. Husk retained three full-time gardeners.

During World War II, it became difficult to continue to garden on a large scale. At this time the purpose of the Husk garden shifted to the creation of a Victory garden; a large portion of the backyard was devoted to vegetables, and the formal beds in the center of the yard were removed. The gardens flanking the border of the property

remained, as well as the *parterres* in the hedged garden space behind the neighboring house.

Like many other High Street homes, The Miltmore-Husk property retained its service area directly behind the house. Wooden arbors led from the back to a small drying yard and wood storage area divided by a fence from the larger open yard. Some of the architectural features such as fences, a summerhouse, and an inviting wooden garden archway remain on the property although most of the central gardens have been returned to lawn and most of the original pleasure garden area has been adapted for modern-day life.

Today, tidy front and side yards frame the handsome house. An attractive pool and patio area in the backyard are backed by old rhododendron, yews, and an ancient gnarled apple tree. Property lines are still marked by towering old pines, dogwood, azaleas, and a variety of other deciduous trees and flowering shrubs. A white summerhouse still caps the hill at the end of the property. Beds of old hostas, ferns, lilies, iris, and phlox add summer color. A winged euonymus hedge provides the boundaries of a secret garden for the rose and ivy bordered playhouse built on the land behind the neighboring house. No longer a formal garden, it waits for a new generation of children to play within its borders.

*William G. Perry, Thomas M. Shaw, and Andrew H. Hepburn as shown in* Williamsburg Before and After: The Rebirth of Virginia's Colonial Capital.

Toward the close of the nineteenth century, influential architects and landscape architects began to recognize Newburyport's significant collection of houses, gardens, fences, and garden structures from the early years of the century and celebrated their survival in writings, photographs, and drawings. Arthur Shurcliff, the noted landscape architect for Colonial Williamsburg, featured the Brockway garden at 83–85 High Street as a colonial New England garden in an 1899 article for *New England Monthly*. Perry, Shaw, and Hepburn, the architects for Colonial Williamsburg, published plans of many High Street gardens in the Garden Club of America publication, *Gardens of Colony and State*. William Perry's mother, Georgianna, was among a group of High Street enthusiasts who revived the Newburyport Horticultural Exhibitions to raise funds to beautify the new High School grounds. The exhibition featured samples of plants, 100 year-old trees, collections of old roses from Newburyport gardens, fruits, perennials and other favorites that fostered an appreciation of Newburyport's horticultural legacies. She is listed as Chairman of the Historic Gardens Committee for Newburyport, and presumably coordinated the writing about Newburyport's gardens for *Gardens of Colony and State*.

William Perry featured High Street's architectural and landscape legacy in his introduction to the *Architectural Heritage of the Merrimack* written by John Mead Howells. These gardens were documented by the Historic American Buildings Survey (HABS) in the 1930s, undoubtedly at the urging of Perry who was influential in shaping the HABS program, and had retained his mother's home on High Street as a summer residence. Robert Cram, whose photographs accompany the plans in *Gardens of Colony and State*, was an up-and-coming landscape architect and professor at Harvard's design school who died before the book was published.

Arthur Shurcliff, Robert Cram, and William Perry identified the High Street properties as the "true products of colonial New England." Newburyport had much older houses at the time they wrote these articles, but it is the High Street properties, with their gardens dating to the 1830s and 1840s, which were celebrated as "ancient colonial gardens." When Shurcliff wrote his article for the 1932 George Washington Bicentennial Commissions' publication, he noted that Salem, Marblehead, Newburyport, and other New England communities were "…typical in possessing Colonial places which have come down to us from the time of Washington with some of the ancient glamour of interest and charm still clinging to them."

Their popularity encouraged preservation of these properties throughout the twentieth century. Many have been lost, but a remarkable number have survived, and have been proudly celebrated, often to the detriment of the older, more historic properties of Newburyport. Writing about High Street in an introduction to the 1931 Historical Society of Old Newbury House Tour brochure, author John Marquand writes:

> Despite the unfortunate interpolation of a later period—very little building here has been good since the early 1800s—this street represents probably better than any other New England street, not excepting Portsmouth and Salem, the wealth and cultivation of that transient but most amazing epoch in American history, the Federalist era.

The Colonial Revival garden arch marks the intersection of two garden paths as seen in this hand colored glass-lantern slide.

*The playhouse in its garden setting where Deirdre Heersink celebrated her sixth birthday in 1979 with her big sister Meghan and friends Sage and Emily Chandler.*

PART THREE

*Public Spaces*

# PUBLIC SPACES

Early New England settlements of the Massachusetts Bay Colony often set aside common land for communal agricultural use, but it was not until the nineteenth century with its trend toward urban growth that the concept of space designated specifically for public enjoyment and recreation seized the popular imagination. The classic example is Central Park, in New York City, constructed by Frederick Law Olmsted and Calvert Vaux. Both the Bartlet Mall and the Atkinson Common in Newburyport succeed in fulfilling the main precepts of early American parks —public access, retention of space following the natural principles of landscape design, and preservation of the spirit of rural tranquility.

*(Opposite) An old view of the Mall* allée. *The* allée *has recently been replanted.*

The courthouse facing the head of Green Street was designed by Charles Bulfinch and completed in 1805. Unlike today's courthouse, the original had a front colonnade with brick pillars and arches supporting the second story. A relief of a female figure holding in her hand a pair of scales representing Justice centered a large upper story pediment. The courthouse was remodeled in 1853, after the town voted to sell all its interest in the building. Ownership was turned over to Essex County. The front arches were closed, the figure of Justice removed, and the old roof taken down and replaced by a new one with heavy cornices and brackets.

# THE BARTLET MALL

The first parcel that was designated as common land in Newburyport is now a public park, with a tree-lined promenade fronting High Street. Although it has also been called Washington Park, it is generally known as the Bartlet Mall, pronounced locally with a flat a, as in "pal." Technically, a mall is a shaded walk or public promenade. This type of space lies within the park, but in recent times the entire property has come to be known as the Bartlet Mall. Shaped by an ancient glacier, the area surrounds a geologic kettlehole that includes a large Frog Pond speckled with lily pads. The mall was originally used during the seventeenth century as common grazing land for sheep and other livestock. More public uses evolved after the town selectmen in 1766 suggested that its acreage be laid out "for the use of the town." Soon there was a ropewalk where hemp was twisted into cordage for ships, a powder house for manufacturing saltpeter, a potter's kiln, a turpentine distillery, a windmill, hay scales, and a "Trayning Field" for the use of militia companies. The Old Hill Burying Ground was laid out on the southwesterly side in 1729, and the community jail was constructed nearby in 1824. Schools were also built within its borders.

In 1799, merchant Nathaniel Tracy received permission to plant shade trees where the ropewalk had originally been constructed but was no longer in use. A year later, an invitation circulated by the town, requested "all interested persons … come with shovel and hoe to help grade and, lay out terraces and a walk and set out trees." Twenty-five-year-old Captain Edmund Bartlet and some friends volunteered to improve the area by filling in the deep ravine at the head of Green Street and by cleaning up the Frog Pond common area. At that time, a broad promenade was laid out paralleling High Street. Bartlet's contribution of $1,400 toward improvements in the common property led the townspeople to name the grounds in his honor. In 1802, perhaps in thanks for his generosity, a poem dedicated to Captain Bartlet was published in the *Newburyport Herald and Country Gazette*. The verses included:

> "So in the Mall the blooming Belle,
> Her charms confess'd to view;
> Now sucks the lip, now waves the curl
> And bids the beau pursue."

In 1805, a courthouse was built between the shaded walkway and the Frog Pond. Originally designed by Bulfinch, it lost much of his signature style when the building was remodeled in 1853. More recently, in the 1970s, part of the old Courthouse was blown up in a gesture of social protest. The property played an important role in the celebratory life of the city in the nineteenth century, serving as the center for Independence Day and other

*Early view of the Bartlet Mall*

*Views of the Bartlet Mall and Frog Pond.*

celebrations. In the summer of 1817, President James Monroe visited Newburyport. At the Mall, "the President passed under a civic arch, decorated with flowers, and along each side, were arranged forming a living avenue, one thousand eight hundred and fifty children, chiefly pupils of the public schools of the town and vicinity. From the front of the Court House, hung a flag which had been borne in the battles of the Revolution." In 1838, a town subscription to grade and ornament the westerly end of the mall brought further improvements.

Later in the nineteenth century, when conditions around the Frog Pond and the Mall had severely deteriorated, a group of concerned people formed the Bartlet Mall Improvement Society to regrade and improve the Mall promenade and the surrounding public grounds. The Society chose Charles Eliot, a Cambridge, Massachusetts landscape architect, to submit a design that would improve the property. In a description of the commission, Eliot wrote, "You are determined that your ancient common shall be made more useful and attractive than it ever yet has been as a promenard (sic) for the grown folks of your City and as a playground for the children of the schools." Although there was not sufficient money allocated to complete the architect's entire plan, Eliot's improvements were considered very successful. The design included a new promenade along Pond Street, a gravel beach bordering the Frog Pond, construction of several flights of steps leading down the steep embankments to the level of the beach, and additional paths and plantings further connecting the property. In 1891, Edward Strong Moseley presented a decorative swan fountain for the Frog Pond to the City in memory of his father, Ebenezer Moseley, who had been involved in the original Bartlet Mall improvements in the early 1800s. In 1935, landscape architect Arthur A. Shurcliff was contacted to modify the landscape of the Mall again. Unfortunately, few of his proposed changes were carried out. Recently, the Newburyport Park Commission planted an *alleé* of hybrid American Elms along the original Bartlet promenade, replicating Charles Eliot's vision of the land adjacent to High Street.

Today the park is used mainly as a resting-place for peaceful contemplation or as a promenade for walkers and joggers. Children slide down the steep slopes in the winter and skaters enjoy the pond. To casual passers-by, it is especially pleasant as a green spot in the midst of a busy city.

*The Bartlet Mall before the fountain was installed.*
*(Inset) 1887 plan of the Bartlet Mall by landscape designer Charles Eliot.*

PRELIMINARY SKETCH
SHOWING PROPOSED IMPROVEMENT
OF THE
OLD COMMON
NEWBURYPORT MASS.

PARK ST BOSTON
30 SEPT 1887
CHARLES ELIOT
LANDSCAPE ARCHT.

SCALE

## High Street Drinking Fountains

In the mid-nineteenth century, when horses were still the transport of the day, and a smart team and handsome carriage the equivalent of today's luxury car, the on-street drinking fountain to water horses was as necessary to town life as gas stations are today. In 19th century Newburyport, there were three High Street fountains, two donated as memorials.

The fountain at High and Auburn Street, near the westerly end of the Bartlet Mall, was formally presented to the city in September, 1898, by Ann E. Taggard, of East Boston, in memory of her husband, Cyrus H. Taggard (below).

The fountain at the corner of High and Toppan's Lane, near Mount Rural, was presented to the city by Paul A. Merrill. It was placed into position in August 1897.

The fountain (left) at the junction of Storey Avenue, Moseley Avenue, and Ferry Road, across the street from Atkinson Common, was the gift of John T. Brown in memory of his wife Ellen T. Brown. It was dedicated in August 1894, and can be seen today.

*Taggard Memorial Fountain at the corner of High Street and Auburn. Only the cement base remains.*

(Above) Quotation found on fountain near Atkinson common.
(Left and top) Circa 1921 photographs show the remnants of the fountain at Toppan's Lane and High Street near Mt. Rural. William G. Dodge poses with his horse and carriage next to his house, which is seen in the photograph at left.

# Newburyport Trees

- Public tree planting in Newburyport was said to begin in March, 1799, when successful merchant and horticultural enthusiast Nathaniel Tracy was authorized by the town fathers to plant trees on High Street. Trees were authorized for the Mall as well. The Mall was improved again by tree plantings supplied by the town in 1838 and in 1853.

- By 1853, there were approximately 1150 shade trees lining both sides of High Street from Marlboro Street to the three road junction near Atkinson Common. Old photographs show that most were American elms.

- The first ornamental tree imported to the United States was the Lombardy poplar. In 1803, when Newburyport merchants built the Newburyport turnpike that extended to Boston, they lined the turnpike with Lombardy poplars from its starting point on High Street to Parker Street, which is close to a mile away.

- In 1850, John Bromfield left a bequest of $10,000 to Newburyport, half of the interest accruing to be spent annually "in planting and preserving trees on the public streets of Newburyport for embellishment and ornamentation of said streets for the pleasure and comfort of its inhabitants."

- In 1873, 65 street trees were planted; in 1880, 26 sugar maples were added to the plantings on Atkinson Common; in 1897, notes show that the committee recommended protecting the trees from mischievous boys and irresponsible horses; in 1898, 84 more trees were planted.

*"A Partial History of Tree Planting in Newburyport," an unpublished paper by F.P. Bailey, a member of the Newburyport City Improvement Society, was written in the 1960s and is presently in the archives of the Newburyport Public Library. The paper notes public tree plantings that extend from 1799 throughout the nineteenth century*

*(Clockwise from upper left) Beech tree at 47 High Street. The twisted unicorn-horn-shaped branch was probably formed by pressure from a bittersweet vine. Silk tree (Acacia) at 89–91 High Street. Smoke tree (Cotinus coggyria) at 89–91 High Street. Silverbell tree (Halesia) at 67 High Street (behind 63 High).*

# ATKINSON COMMON

Atkinson Common lies on the north side of High Street, near the three-road junction of Moseley and Storey Avenues and the Ferry Road. At one time, this area marked the northern boundary of the town. The original approximately eight-acre property was given to the city by Mrs. Eunice Atkinson Currier in 1873 in memory of her father, Matthias Atkinson. This land was gradually augmented by purchases of contiguous acreage by the Belleville Improvement Society. Over the years, the Common has evolved into an unusual blend of historic structures, commemorative monuments, and elaborate gardens.

The donated fields lay untouched until a neighborhood group formed to convert the uncultivated land into a public park and garden for the residents of Newburyport's Belleville neighborhood in the western section of the city. In 1894, the Belleville Improvement Society began the process of overseeing the design and layout of trees, shrubs, beds, drives, and walks in the picturesque and elaborate manner of the day, gradually transforming the open fields into a Victorian park. The Society continues to advocate for the Common.

The park is organized along a central north-south axis, and is composed of three major areas, or "rooms." Its commemorative aspect was introduced in the first area with the dedication in 1902 of a handsome bronze statue of a Civil War veteran. In 1913, stone tablets were added inscribed with President Lincoln's Gettysburg address and the names of Newburyport soldiers and sailors who served in that war. These tablets were placed near the second major "room," which focuses upon a graceful central lily pond originally spanned by a decorative wooden arched bridge. The third area includes the present rusticated stone tower. It stands on the same central axis far beyond the pond on the escarpment that once overlooked the Merrimack River and the town. Today, mature trees block the view seen in former days.

There have been changes in structure, design, and location of park furnishings during the more than a century of their existence. In 1929, the wooden bridge over the lily pond was replaced by one fashioned of iron. Originally, a wooden arbor straddled the main axis behind the lily pond, while the first tower, in the same rustic wooden style as the early bridge and the present original wooden gazebo, stood at the end of a long pine grove on the northwest side of the park. By 1935, the wooden arbor as well as the wooden tower were removed. The tower was replaced by one of rusticated stone built by the Works Projects Administration (WPA). Its location at the northeast end of the central axis of the Common extended the landscaped area. The tower also provided a new visual landmark to

*This pine alleé once led to the first wooden tower built at Atkinson Common.*

Bridge and Observation Tower, Atkinson Park, Newburyport, Mass

the city, as it was visible from High Street. The stone toilet building, also built by the WPA, brought attention to an entrance near Plummer Avenue which was added to the park about 1910. This entrance became even more popular in 1973, with the addition of tennis courts in that area. A commemorative obelisk was added to the main axis in 1951 between the pond and the tower.

In 1935, the Belleville Improvement Society purchased more contiguous land from the Merrill estate and deeded that additional property to the city. Today, that section of Atkinson Common bordering Merrimack Street is called Pioneer Field and is the site of the city's baseball and softball fields.

The curvilinear pond remains flanked by the asymmetrically placed gazebo and by informally spaced plant materials that emphasize the less formal aspects of the picturesque style. Pedestrians stroll past both massed and specimen plantings that include evergreens and deciduous trees, flowering shrubs and occasional elaborate and colorful flower beds. Pines, hemlocks, arborvitae, showy weeping spruce, yew, and false cyprus remain from the early period; some are original components of an early topiary garden behind the gazebo, others are part of a conifer garden or long-established groves. A grouping of weeping mulberries also remains.

A capital campaign to benefit the park began in 2000. The ability to reference a new master plan for the property helped the governing society to focus on a phased improvement schedule with the broad and ambitious goal of "restoring and renewing" Atkinson Common. Presently, the path systems have been reworked, and trees, shrubs and flower beds augmented or pruned. Memorial benches, irrigation, and a new circulating system for the lily pool have been installed. Although the original overall plan has been simplified for contemporary use and maintenance, the historic character of the park has been carefully preserved. Its evocative monuments to a long-ago war combine with the shadowed dignity of mature trees to provide a unique and peaceful landscape for those who stroll its paths.

The Civil War monument presides over the park.

PART FOUR

*New Gardens*
*in Old Spaces*

# NEW GARDENS IN OLD SPACES

Fine-tuning an established garden or designing and constructing a new one continues to be a popular project for families living on High Street today. The Perkins family in the Ebenezer Greenleaf House at 87 High Street is adapting their evolving garden space to family living. Its previous owners, Nancy Kirk Beasley and Robert S. Miller, contributed to its present charm. Julia Farwell-Clay has returned a terraced garden to 203 High Street, one of the oldest homes on the street, after a disappearance that extended for almost two centuries.

*(Above) The lattice summerhouse at 87 High Street is a focal point of the garden space.*
*(Opposite) Hollyhocks enhance the back entry way at 87 High Street.*
*(Left) Fancywork in an early photograph at 87 High Street, since removed.*

## 87 High Street
# GREENLEAF WOOD PERKINS HOUSE

Newburyport merchant Ebenezer Greenleaf was the first to built his house on this section of the High Street ridge. It was completed in 1799, and he sold the neighboring lot to the Moultons in 1809. His widow, Jane Coombs Greenleaf, remained on the property for the next forty years. Since then, many owners have left their stamp on the landscape. William Perkins, the present occupant, is a Coombs descendent. He, his wife Maura, and their two children have already made their mark in the garden, building on what was already there.

Similar in tone to the flanking lots, the front of the property is plain, even stark, enlivened only by traditional border plantings and a 50-year old blue spruce, added to bring privacy to rooms in a stepped-back ell. The house stands on its own, porch railing and fence lending a sense of motion to the quiet space. The original balustrade above the porch was removed by a former owner.

Behind the house, the well-established shrub borders draw immediate attention to the privacy and boundaries of the yard. The proximity of neighboring properties is camouflaged by a dense hemlock hedge on the left, balanced by an old-fashioned shrub border on the right. Its lilacs, hydrangeas, mock oranges, and forsythia are in keeping with varieties listed in an early Moulton garden plan, and they bring color to the spring landscape. Both garden and yard have changed over time with the shifting configuration of the house and the growth of the trees. Porches have been added then removed, and the last owner, Robert S. Miller, did an extensive renovation of the property, including an addition to the rear of the original house. Near a small back porch, trellises support a rose and clematis. Fronted by spring bulbs, summer hollyhocks, and fall dahlias, the area benefits from reflected sun in every season. A multi-stemmed American Linden and a sugar maple dominate the right side of the yard, providing dappled shade to both grass and nearby shrub beds. Perhaps encroaching shade contributed to a long-ago decision to remove a garden bed from the right side of the central path. The large one hundred-year-old maple grows close to the rear of the house, providing summer shade and winter interest. A ring of hosta around its trunk is surrounded by a broad circle of old bricks, a byway in the boxwood-edged central path system that leads to house, gardens, summerhouse, and play area. Some of the boxwood was originally grown in the garden across the street at the Cushing House.

The formal garden lies behind the carriage house, to the left of the main path. Lilacs and buddlea, hollies and peonies soften its corner location. Old bricks again set the tone. This

*The summerhouse in the middle of the garden is a copy of one that once stood next door at the Moulton House.*

*(Top) The swing set and chaises create a comfortable outdoor family environment. (Bottom) A mature white hawthorne in full bloom at the rear of the property.*

time they form three large concentric circles. The center of the first is divided into a pie shape and overflows with a variety of herbs. The center circle features a sundial; its surrounding bed is bright with low miniature roses. The third circle is solid brick; a table and chairs shaded by an umbrella offer a pleasant spot for lunch or a respite from gardening. Beds framing the circles include a variety of traditional perennials and rose varieties, including an old-fashioned nineteenth century white shrub rose brought from the garden of Mr. Miller's mother in Ithaca, New York.

The white latticed summerhouse is a focal point of the garden space. In the right border of the property stands the back of the Moulton summerhouse at 89–91 High Street. The one standing parallel at the head of the garden in the Perkins' yard is a replica of a second Moulton summerhouse, missing since its disintegration many years ago. The approximately forty-year-old present copy is exact, save for the roof that was originally latticed rather than shingled. To the right is a bed of annuals providing continual summer color.

Similar to many of the other High Street houses, the far end of the expansive rear yard was once an orchard. Garden chairs, swings, and a slide have replaced the cherry trees that were present until the last decade. Removal of an established cedar grove brightens the back lawn and its backdrop of rhododendrons and azaleas, a large white hawthorn, and towering spruce and pine. Woods lie beyond. On the right, the rear yard is partially bisected by a spruce hedge ending in a shrub bed. It gives shape to a "secret garden," installed by a previous owner.

Although the property is old, there are no historic remnants of an original garden. Despite this, the long narrow prototypical High Street lot exudes the fascination of a well-loved, planned, and cared for traditional garden space. It is especially endearing as it melds the old with the new in a charming and well-integrated manner. The garden is also appealing, as it is in a state of growth and change that is typical of a vital work-in-progress. The warmth and soft edges of this garden combine with recent practical changes and adaptations to create a comfortable and manageable family space.

*The current owners shingled the open lattice roof of this summerhouse. Note the dense hedge dividing the property from its neighbor to the east.*

## 203 High Street
# LOWELL TRACY JOHNSON FARWELL-CLAY

Julia Farwell-Clay was initially attracted to the Lowell Tracy Johnson House, one of the earliest homes built on the street, in 1998, because of its classic architecture and its centuries-long presence in the city. When she realized there was no established garden her interest grew, for she considered its purchase an opportunity to put down both figurative and literal roots. She and her husband were immediately drawn to the old trees: in the front, an enormous sugar maple, a towering linden, and mature Japanese maples; at the back, ancient gnarled pears that flank the path at the far end of the first terrace. The pears have brought them a small connection to the past. Their neighbor in the next door Jackson Dexter Kelley Quill House grew up in Newburyport and told them that during his Huck Finn summers of sampling every pear tree in town, the Seckels from their trees were the best. Julia has read that the Marquis de Lafayette, a guest of the Lowell family, admired the extensive orchards then on the property. She likes to think of her pears as descendants of those originals.

Lucinda Brockway's lecture about High Street gardens during the Newburyport Garden Symposium inspired Julia to attempt a garden that has the spirit of that tradition and legacy—not a reproduction of an historic Newburyport garden, but rather a kind of tribute to it. During construction, the grass surrendered clues to gardens and structures that had been there before. They found brick lined cisterns as they dug the foundation for the new patio and discovered that the strange slopes in the lawn were not accidental, but the eroded remains of terraces carved from the gentle hill. The soil was free of rocks except where the terraces dipped to the next level. They excavated broken crockery, bottle shards, and chunks of coal. An ancient logic lay hidden by the grass; here had been a tended garden, their "not garden." As they reclaimed the wild lower lawn, Julia found a tenacious asparagus frond, joyful proof that here had lived a gardener. Here had been his vegetable bed!

The new garden moves down a series of terraces that begins directly behind the house with a bricked patio area. A central path passes around an armillary, through a hedge of European beech, past a children's play area, and descends granite steps to a second level. A fieldstone wall and a classic colonnade supporting roses and wisteria is backdrop to a fenced vegetable garden and a boxwood enclosed *parterre* of floribunda and varieties of old garden roses. Further steps descend to the third level, an expanse of lawn for games, fronted by a perennial border that includes lady's mantle, hollyhocks, red hot poker, euphorbia, and smoke bush. Another drop at the far end of the lawn leads to a wild meadow, and beyond, mature trees and untamed undergrowth. Julia says she has not yet found

*(Opposite) The new gardens delineate, through their terracing, the topography of the rear yard.*

a place for a garden house, but thinks perhaps this new garden has no proper claims to one. Maybe, she remarks, when she is an old woman, she will build it where she most wants to rest from her weeding.

The long history of the house is filled with stories and personalities. In 1771, recent Harvard graduates John Lowell and Jonathan Jackson combined resources to buy five acres of land on High Street. Dividing the property, "each promised to never marry so that no person could come between them." Subsequently, Lowell married twice and Jackson three times. They remained friends throughout their lives, and Jackson's daughter married a Lowell son. John Lowell built his early Federal house on the up-river side of the five acres in 1774 at the time of his second marriage to a Boston Cabot, and four years later sold his property to Patrick Tracy and moved to Boston. Tracy bought the house as a gift for his son John, who remained in the house until 1809.

In 1782, the Marquis de Chastellux visited Newburyport with three other French noblemen: de Vaudreuil, de Tallerand and de Montesquieu. They were entertained by Colonel Wigglesworth and John Tracy at what the Frenchmen described as a "country house." This was John Tracy's High Street home. In a de Chastellux diary entry later quoted in a Newburyport House Tour brochure written by Newburyport author John Marquand, M. de Chastellux describes his evening at the Tracy "country house." It was night when he arrived…. "I went, however, by moonlight to see the garden, which is composed of different terraces. There is likewise a hothouse and a number of young trees. The house is handsome and well finished and everything breathes that air of magnificence, accompanied by simplicity, which is only to be found among merchants. The evening passed rapidly by the aid of agreeable conversation and a few glasses of punch. The ladies we found assembled were Mrs. Tracy, her two sisters, and their cousin, Miss Lee. Mrs. Tracy has an agreeable and sensible countenance and her manners correspond with her appearance. At ten o'clock an excellent supper was served. We drank good wine; Miss Lee sung, and prevailed upon Messrs. de Vaudreuil and de Talleyrand to sing also. Toward midnight the ladies withdrew, but we continued drinking Madeira and Xery. Mr. Tracy, according to the custom of the country, offered us pipes, which were accepted by M. de Talleyrand and M. de Montesquieu, the consequence of which was

that they became intoxicated and were led home, where they were happy to go to bed. As to myself, I remained perfectly cool and continued to converse on trade and politics with Mr. Tracy."

In 1809, the property was bought by Eleazer Johnson. In his earlier years, Johnson was one of the band of patriots who burned tea on the Newburyport docks during an anti-tax demonstration predating the more famous Boston tea party. The house remained in his family until the middle of the twentieth century. Gradually, over time, the gardens constructed by the Tracys vanished. They are rumored to be the first terraced gardens in Newburyport. Only a few of the early trees survived. In 2000, the present owner began to plan her campaign to return the garden to its early beauty. Today, the garden is one of the best on High Street. It recaptures the spirit of the nineteenth century pleasure garden, while interpreting it in the style of the twenty-first.

*The colonnade creates a shady resting place in the garden.*

*The armillary stands on a pink granite mill stone. Inset: The picket fence encloses the raised-bed vegetable garden.*

*Fall foliage enhances the architectural detail of 203 High Street.*

## PART FIVE

*History in
Your Own Backyard*

# HISTORY IN YOUR OWN BACKYARD

## by Lucinda Brockway

William Hoskins, the noted English cultural geographer likened the landscape to a symphony—understood for its larger themes, but better appreciated for the individual melodies that wind their way throughout the entire work. I like to think of garden design in the same way. When broken into its various elements, some large and some small, we can better understand what makes any garden a beautiful, complete work. Whether a garden is new or old, it possesses similar *structural* characteristics. It is the *design influence* that defines the arrangement of these pieces as a product of their era. We are anxious to define a garden as Victorian, or Colonial or Colonial Revival. What we are really speaking about is the design philosophy of each era. All gardens share similar elements (walls, hedges, trees, shrubs, paths, garden beds), but it is the artistic arrangement of these elements that determines its period. Technology played a huge role in garden contents. With each of these design periods comes an understanding that tools, decorative arts, and plants were introduced at specific times in American history and shaped the look of the garden. The lawn mower, for example, profoundly affected our ability and our desire for a perfect greensward around our homes in the nineteenth century. Home irrigation systems allowed us to keep it green, despite the heat of summer. The car needed a place to park; iron garden furniture replaced the old kitchen chair that found its way into the garden; Lewis and Clark brought back a myriad of plants previously unknown to East Coast gardens before the early nineteenth century. Each of these events shaped the opportunities and products available to American gardeners, and changed the look of their own back yards.

As we delve into the process of garden rejuvenation, there are several active steps you can take in the long-range preparation to establish your garden:

## Step 1: Get Outside and Document the Details

Look, look and look again. Take lots of pictures. Get to know the garden in intimate detail, like discovering the past history of your new best friend. This will help to shape your thinking, and your garden planning. Watch and document the garden through all seasons. Learn about the property in detail—bones, framework and frosting. Document it in every way that you can. A plan done to scale (¼", ⅛", ¹⁄₁₆" etc.) is the best means of generating a plan from which you can build future designs. This can be drawn on sheets of graph paper purchased at the local art supply store, or you can hire a professional surveyor to do the job. Some of the best evidence we have for the Moulton garden and the

*Captain Shuff House, 187 High Street, demonstrates the remnants of an earlier garden plan. Flowering shrubs line parts of the surviving path that passes by old fruit trees on its way to the summerhouse.*

# Elements of Design

**Bones.** The structural framework or "skeleton" of the garden. These elements are the most durable and survive the longest. The garden's bones consist of its topography, its stone walls, stone paths, long lived specimen trees, and any of the elements that provide the basic structure of the space, made of materials that survive over generations. Sometimes the bones include strong axial alignments, views, and patterns on the landscape that are not eroded over time. Sometimes the bones are only visible at key times of the year, when foliage does not obscure their existence or drought brings these features to the surface. Even when they are obscured by overgrowth, the sweep of a brick walk leading from the house to the privy can be uncovered beneath years of leaf mold. Stonewalls march their way through New England woodlands, framing earlier farm fields. "Ghost" paths and building foundations emerge through the lawn when the heat of summer dries out the green grass covering their surface.

*The ghost paths of the 1910 garden appeared during periods of summer drought. Gardens of the Pell family, Fort Ticonderoga, NY.*

**Frame.** The elements that shape the spaces with the garden that are less durable than the garden's bones. Like our own cartilage and muscle, these elements define the form and shape of the landscape, but can be shed or deteriorate over time. They include things like wooden fences, arbors, pergolas, hedges, mixed boundary plantings, and most small trees, shrubs and vines.

**Frosting.** These elements are the most fleeting within the landscape, but often the most memorable. Like clothing, they provide the color and texture of the garden, and change with each season or each owner's personal taste. They include the bulbs, annuals, perennials and biennials within the garden beds, decorative pots, urns and furnishings. The frosting includes the sounds and smells in the garden—as fleeting as a single moment—like water spilling over rocks, the first blush of spring crocuses, and the last gasp of fall foliage.

Any garden, in any period, includes these elements. Collectively, they shape and define individual spaces. How they are arranged, what materials are used, and how well they age are a product of their time, their quality of construction, and the success of the spatial design and plant selection.

Categorizing these elements is easy, coming to understand them well is more difficult. It takes years of experience to read all of the bones in a badly deteriorated garden. It takes good design skills to create memorable frosting. It takes great construction skills to build bones and framework that will last. Above all else, however, there are three factors that have the strongest influence on any garden: Weather, Nature and Good Maintenance. Winter storms, hurricanes and tornadoes have the most spectacular effects on the landscape, but it is the seasonal regularity of pests, disease, animal damage, drought and too much rain that take the biggest toll. Poor maintenance can destroy a good garden quicker than any summer storm or insect plague. So you see, modern gardens and historic gardens are not much different. They all share the same cycles, the same elements, and the same dedication to good maintenance.

What about this process of historic garden design? How can the gardens in this book work for you? If you are beginning a garden design with a blank slate, you have fewer steps required in the research process. However, is there really ever a totally blank slate? Every new property is carved out of one that came before. Every property includes specific soils, topography, drainage and mini climates that come with the "blank slate." Getting to know what came before is both interesting and critical to best understand each property under consideration for garden improvements.

If you have an existing garden, or the wild remains of a former garden, you have a little more work to do in gathering information prior to doing a good plan. Though this takes some time, the joy is in the discovery, and the information you glean provides great stories when you can finally entertain in your restored garden. For what is a garden if it doesn't have its share of stories to tell? The National Park Service, your local Historical Commission, The National Trust for Historic Preservation, or your State Historic Preservation Office have lots of publications available to help guide you through the process of working with historic landscapes. More and more professionals are available that can work with you to research, design and rejuvenate your landscape or garden. But the process can be something you learn for yourself. It takes time, patience, humility and a lot of pointed questions to rejuvenate an existing garden, or design your own period-inspired landscape.

Cushing House garden came from sketches that gardeners drew of their garden and its contents. Even though these were not to scale, the scale of the drawing was inferred from its design because the "bones" and the "frame" of these gardens still remained intact

Mark on the plan all of the features that you see, including plants, buildings, paths, utilities, and "ghost features" that appear only at certain seasons of the year. Photograph everything you mark on your plan. Look for clues indicating change: changes in grade, a build up of soils, "settling" of buildings. Dying grass during a drought can reveal old road systems, paths, building foundations, and other "ghost" features. Compost heaps produce generations of garden plants where extras were thrown away. Trees and shrubs can offer clues to old roads, hedges, and pruning patterns. Stonewalls, ditches, fences and drains teach field patterns, changes in land use, and sometimes can even reveal how the fields were used. Pasture pines and trees with broad, spreading crowns in the middle of woodlands are indicator trees for former pastures and open fields.

Plants tell their own stories. Changes in the landscape can be read through the introduction dates for existing plants. Combined with our native species are an abundance of plants brought to this country from around the world. Many were popularized as they were introduced—the "hot" plants on the market innovative gardeners had to have. Remnants of wooden benches, arbors, irrigation systems (i.e. water spigots), ponds, steps, terraces, garden edgings, and other garden features offer more intimate details about gardens and grounds.

## Step 2: Search for Clues in All the Right Places

This step takes you from the garden into the attic, nearest library or courthouse. Collect any and all information you can about:

- Who lived here?
- Who did they know? Where did their family and friends live?
- When did the land change hands? To whom?
- Did they have help in designing or tending the land?
- Was the space around them used for work, pleasure or "wilderness"?
- What changes were made to the building(s)? When?
- Did the size of the property or garden change? What and where were the boundaries?
- What did the place look like? How did it relate to its surroundings?

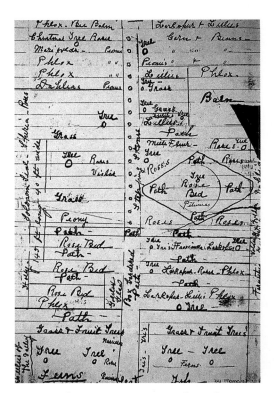

*Drawing by Miss Margaret Cushing depicting her memory of the garden layout at 98 High Street during her childhood. The garden's most recent restoration was based on this plan.*

Answers to these and other questions can come from land deeds, probate records, family papers, census records, tax and assessor's records, maps, birds eye views, aerials, newspapers, town records, court records, photographs, paintings, engravings, drawings, professional records, farm records, and oral histories. Where can you find them? Town historical societies, town offices (tax collector records and planning offices), county courthouses (land evidence records/ deeds and probate records), state archives, state historical societies, Library of Congress, private libraries and personal collections.

If there was a battle fought near your property, check for any maps and plans drawn by military scouts and cartographers before and after the battle. These are often extremely detailed with regards to landscape information. If your home was a seasonal residence for a particular family, check with the libraries and record offices where their primary residence was located. Check professional landscape architects records for homeowner's names related to your property. Federal census records for the nineteenth century include detailed

*Steps formerly part of the Pike Cushing Bernhome property. The garden is now gone but the bones remain.*

inventories of farms and industries—invaluable if your property was in active agriculture or included a small industrial operation. Obviously, post cards, photographs and aerial photographs are invaluable sources of information. These can be found in local libraries, historical societies, or private collections. The Historic American Buildings Survey, whose records are now housed within the Library of Congress, is a wonderful resource for plans and photographs. Many of the plans and some of the old photographs in this book came from this archive. These records are now available over the Internet. Similarly, records for the National Register, National Landmark programs, and other inventories and surveys of historic resources may include information about your property. These can be found through the state historic preservation office.

TerraServer and other aerial or satellite imagery sites offer recent aerial views of your property on the Internet. Some college and private libraries have historic map and photograph collections available for search on line. Start by searching for your town, then by family name or street address. Please be aware that street addresses may

change so double check the exact location of the property as you do your research. Ask everyone questions, and seek as much information as you can. Often, one good source will lead to another. Don't be discouraged. Find as much as you can about your property, then collect information about similar, nearby properties. Often these sites can be used as context for decisions you make about your own property.

Organize all of the historic information in a loose-leaf notebook. Organize your notes by date, by owner, or by type of information (pictures, deeds, letters, probate, etc.)—whatever method suits you best. The notebook is never complete, and as additional information is found, it can easily be added. Research is never done. Don't forget to add a section for the pictures, plans and photographs of the property as you take them—these form your historical record for the next generation.

Together, all of these little bits of information combine to tell a big story. Look, listen, question, seek the answers, and then begin to put the pieces in place like the pieces to a jigsaw puzzle. Sometimes you will be missing a piece, but the overall picture can still be revealed with one or two pieces missing.

Finally, sort and organize your information from Step 1 and Step 2. See if you can begin to tell a story about this garden, its people, and its contents. Often, as you find historic information, you return outside to see what is there now, and vice versa. You will probably not have all of the answers, but try and piece together everything that you can. Is there one time period that you have lots of information for? Is there one person who was critical to shaping the garden above all others? Do you have a lot of things on site today that most relate to an earlier period?

## Step 3: With All This Information, Where Do You Want to Go?

Learning the history of the property is only the beginning. It brings us to a crossroads, where paths lead into the future based on the decisions you make today. Don't stall in the crossroads and never move forward —stagnation can only go in one direction: Nature will take charge and fashion the property in its own way. Now is the time for lots of discussion. It is the time for clear thinking and careful decision making.

The National Park Service has developed standards for determining the appropriate direction to take with historic landscapes. Often these standards are most applicable to public properties, but their guidelines serve to inform local historical commissions and homeowners in appropriate directions to take with your own property. The Park Service breaks these decisions into four carefully defined directions: restore, reconstruct, rehabilitate and preserve. These words define an attitude and a direction for making decisions, based on the amount of documentary and physical evidence that exists for any property. These terms are very similar, and sometimes difficult to get your arms around with regard to an ever-changing landscape ecosystem, but they are important to consider as you plan your own garden.

"*Preservation*" of a landscape means keeping all of the existing elements that characterize a property today. "*Rehabilitation*" refers to retaining the historic elements of a property, but adding new elements that provide for contemporary use, such as the addition of a new driveway, front walk, patio, swings or other everyday features of modern life. "*Restoration*" means that the property is brought back to its appearance during a specific, earlier era. This includes the removal of elements added since the restoration date, and the addition of missing elements. "*Reconstruction*" refers to putting back missing pieces, when substantial information exists to accurately rebuild these elements. This term is often used when little or no physical evidence remains, but the documentary evidence is so significant that a good reconstruction of the historic garden is possible.

Usually, private landscapes all involve some element of *rehabilitation*, because our needs for the property include things we need for today's living that were not there in an earlier era. However, I have had clients that want to be as period-specific as possible, and with good documentation we have restored or reconstructed historic landscapes to their satisfaction.

Personally, I prefer to think about this entire process as "*rejuvenation*"—breathing new life into something that has aged. Most importantly, know your limitations, and thoroughly understand the maintenance implications of the choices you make. Many homeowners excitedly headed in one direction, only to find that the garden could not be maintained when they got there. A dedication to exceptional, long-term maintenance is critical to any successful landscape project.

For those with a blank slate, I like to think of the design process

as "period" or "period inspired." A "period" landscape or garden is one that has been carefully designed to a specific era. "Period inspired" refers to using the elements of an era in garden design to develop a contemporary interpretation of that period. I have designed landscapes for Victorian houses that were built three years ago, using the principles of landscape design and plant materials popular in the mid-nineteenth century. I have designed landscapes for colonial homes that were completely restored to their 18th century style, using the basic tenets of first period American landscape design. In these cases we did not go back to what had specifically been in place on that site during that period. There either wasn't enough information or the house had been relocated to another prop-

*The beginning of the most recent restoration of the Moulton garden by the current owners. This photograph was taken in 1993.*

*This handsome shade garden was restored after careful research.*

erty. Instead, we designed a landscape that was guided by the principles of the period, and used only plant materials that were available at the time. The photographs and plans in this book can be used to inspire a Federal garden of your own. The garden houses, arrangement of planting beds, path treatments, fences and hedges can define your own interpretation of an early nineteenth century garden.

Bring together what you know about your property today, what you learned in the library, and what your needs are for contemporary living. Use all of this information to build your own "master plan" for your property. This plan is a visual outline of what you want to do, and how you want to get there. If you live in a historic district, you may have to submit your plan for local approvals before you begin. Otherwise, you may want to add to your research notebook your plan, and your reasons for going in that direction. (Again—documentation for future gardeners to enjoy!)

Once you have built your master plan, you can think about how you want to get there. Most often, people cannot do the entire project at once. Old shrubs may need to be rejuvenated. Dead trees may need to be removed. Invasive species, such as honeysuckle, bittersweet, poison ivy and barberry, may have to be removed or brought under control before the "fun" work can begin. Walks may need to be rebuilt, or uncovered, under years of plant debris.

Great gardens take hard work and dedication, so don't wear yourself out in the first year. Take on bite-size pieces that allow you to sit under the shade of that old tree and enjoy what you have accomplished for one year. Develop a phased "to-do" list of work that you want to get done year by year or season by season. Things will always take longer than you think, so be conservative in your lists. As with the house, fix the bones before you move into the frosting—you will never be sorry that you took the time to build the soil, eliminate the invasive plants, fix the old walls, and rejuvenate the old hedgerow before you fill the garden beds with plants.

Finally, remember that landscapes are a constant process of change—growth, death and regeneration. That is what makes them so exciting, and so challenging. Good preservationists, like good gardeners, tolerate the inevitable vagaries of climate, the unpredictable twists and turns of the weather, and the ability for the land to take, tolerate and to give back. They know that they will never know everything. Please, above all, have a good sense of humor, a lot of patience and a huge dose of humility.

Landscape preservation is a subtle guiding of the natural forces that shape our surroundings—an effort to appreciate and understand the land as a combination of form, texture, line, light and shadow in partnership with the biological and chemical science of soils, plants, animals and people. Together, art and science meld into a space that gains its beauty from its past, its present, and its future. Build your own space or refresh an existing one that combines your personality with that of your property. Look. Listen. Learn. Always be a student of the garden.

## "Use it up, wear it out, make it do, or go without."

Newburyport's Yankee merchants and factory owners appreciated the pleasures of the traditional New England ethic of "Use it up, wear it out, make it do, or do without." When the Old South Church on Federal Street was renovated, some of its choicer pieces were incorporated into garden ornaments. The sounding board above the pulpit became the top of the garden house at 49 High Street, while one of the pews became a garden bench at number 89–91, the Moulton House. A tiny model of the church once decorated the top of the spire at the Wheelwright House at 75 High. Pieces of old ships sometimes appeared in gardens: the wooden arch now at the back of the Cushing House garden once housed a ship's figurehead in Miss Nell Todd's garden at 90 High Street. The figurehead is now restored and on exhibit inside the Cushing House.

# Plant List

Note: These plants, referenced in the text, have been documented in Newburyport gardens as they have evolved in the 19th and 20th centuries. Plant lists from HABS drawings and other sources have not been included in this list. This list merely documents plants mentioned within the text of this book, and provides Latin names, where possible, for further clarity in identification.

| COMMON NAME | BOTANICAL NAME | TYPE OF PLANT | COMMON NAME | BOTANICAL NAME | TYPE OF PLANT |
|---|---|---|---|---|---|
| Achyanthus | *Achyranthus splendens* | tropical/houseplant | Forsythia | *Forsythia* cv. | shrub |
| Acuba | *Aucuba japonica* | tropical/houseplant | Foxglove | *Digitalis purpurea* | biennial |
| Adders tongue | *Ophioglossum vulgatum* | perennial | Fraxinella | *Dictamnus albus* | perennial |
| Akebia | *Akebia quinata* | vine | Gaillardia | *Gaillardia grandiflora* | perennial |
| Alyssum | *Lobularia maritima* | annual | Gardenia | *Gardenia* sp. | tropical/houseplant |
| American larch | *Larix laricina* | tree | Geraniums General Grant | | |
| American linden | *Tilia americana* | tree |   & Miss Gertrude | *Pelargonium* x *hortorum* | annual |
| Apple | *Malus* cv. | fruit | Gillyflower | *Dianthus caryophyllus* | perennial |
| Arborvitae; eastern | | | Gladiolus | *Gladiolus* x *hortulanus* | annual |
|   white-cedar; swamp-cedar | *Thuja occidentalis* | tree | Grape-Isabella | *Vitis vinifera Isabella* | vine |
| Azalea | *Rhododendron* cv. | shrub | Grape-Niagara | *Vitis vinifera Niagara* | vine |
| Bachelor buttons | *Centaurea cyanus* | annual | Grape-SalemBlood | *Vitis vinifera Salem Blood* | vine |
| Barberry hedge | *Berberis thunbergii* | shrub | GrapeoDelaware | *Vitis vinifera Delaware* | vine |
| Beans | *Phaseolus* cv. | vegetable | Grape-Rogers | *Vitis vinifera Rogers* | vine |
| Bee Balm | *Monarda didyma* | perennial | Gum tree | *Liquidamber styraciflua* | tree |
| Beech-American | *Fagus grandiflora* | tree | Hawthorne | *Crataegus* sp. | tree |
| Beech-Copper | *Fagus sylvatica* | | Heliotrope | *Heliotropum arborescens* | annual |
| |   var. *atropunicea* | tree | Hellebores | *Helleborus niger* | perennial |
| Beech-English | *Fagus sylvatica* | tree | Hemlock | *Tsuga canadensis* | tree |
| Beech-Purple | *Fagus sylvatica purpurea* | tree | Hibiscus | *Hibiscus syriacus* | shrub |
| Beech-Silver | *Nothofagus menziesii* | tree | Holly berberis | *Mahonia aquifolium* | shrub |
| Bloodroot | *Sanguinaria canadensis* | perennial | Hollyhock | *Alcea rosea* | perennial |
| Boxwood | *Buxus sempervirens* | shrub | Honeysuckle | *Lonicera tatarica* | shrub |
| Butterfly bush | *Buddleia* sp. | shrub | Horse chestnut | *Aesculus carnea* | tree |
| Caladium | *Caladium* sp. | tropical/houseplant | Hosta | *Hosta* sp. | perennial |
| Camellias | *Camellia* sp. | tropical/houseplant | Huskee Peach | *Prunus persica* cv. *Huskee* | fruit |
| Canterbury Bell | *Campanula latifolia* | perennial | Hydrangea | *Hydrangea arborescens* | shrub |
| Cat mint | *Nepeta racemosa* | perennial | Iris | *Iris siberica* or *Iris germanica* | perennial |
| Catalpa | *Catalpa speciosa* | tree | Ivy | *Hedera helix* | vine |
| Cherry | *Prunus* cv. | fruit | Japanese maple | *Acer palmatum* | tree |
| Christmas rose | *Helleborus niger* | perennial | Judas tree | *Cercis canadensis* | tree |
| Chrysanthemum | *Chrysanthemum* cv. | perennial | Kentucky coffeetree | *Gymnocladus dioicus* | tree |
| Clematis | *Clematis* cv. | vine | Knights Spears | *Yucca filamentosa* | perennial |
| Coffee tree | *Gymnocladus dioica* | tree | Goldenraintree | *Koelreuteria paniculata* | tree |
| Coleus (yellow) | *Coleus* cv. | annual | Lady's mantle | *Alchemilla vulgaris* | perennial |
| Columbine | *Aquilegia vulgaris* | perennial | Larkspur | *Consolida orientalis* | annual |
| Crocus | *Crocus vernus* cv. | perennial | Lemon lily | *Hemerocallis flava* | perennial |
| Currant | *Ribes rubrum; Ribes nigrum* | fruit | Lemon verbena | *Lippia citriodora* | annual |
| Daffodil | *Narcissus* sp. | perennial | Lilacs | *Syringa vulgaris* | shrub |
| Dahlia | *Dahlia* cv. | annual | Lilies | *Hemerocallis* sp. & *Lilium* sp. | perennial |
| Daisy | *Chrysanthemum leucanthemum* | perennial | Linden | *Tilia americana* | tree |
| Deutzia | *Deutzia gracilis* | shrub | Lobelia | *Lobelia inflata* | annual |
| Dogwood | *Cornus florida* | tree | Magnolia | *Magnolia* sp. | tree |
| Elm-American | *Ulmus americana* | tree | Maidenhair fern | *Adiantum pedatum* | perennial |
| Elm-English | *Ulmus procera* | tree | Maple-English | *Acer campestre* | tree |
| Elm-purple | *Ulmus carpinifolia purpurea* or | | Maple-Negundo | *Acer negundo* | tree |
| |   *Ulmus glabra atropurpurea* | tree | Maple-Norway | *Acer platanoides* | tree |
| Elm-Weeping | *Ulmus glabra Camperdownii* or | | Maple-Purple | *Acer japonicum* | tree |
| |   *Ulmus parviflora sempervirens* | tree | Maple-Red | *Acer rubrum* | tree |
| Elm-broadleaf | unknown | tree | Maple-Silver | *Acer saccharinu* | tree |
| European barberry | *Berberis vulgaris* | shrub | Maple-Striped | *Acer pennsylvanicum* | tree |
| False cypress | *Chamaecyparis* sp. | tree | Maple-Sugar | *Acer saccharum* | tree |
| Ferns | many varieties | perennial | Marigold | *Tagetes erecta* | annual |
| Flaming Fame bush | *Templetonia retusa* (Flame bush) | shrub | Mignonette | *Reseda odorata* | annual |
| Fleur de lis; Iris | *Iris germanica* | perennial | Mock Orange | *Philadelphus coronarius* | shrub |
| Florida cypress | *Taxodium distichum* | tree | Monkshood | *Aconitum napellus* | perennial |

| COMMON NAME | BOTANICAL NAME | TYPE OF PLANT | COMMON NAME | BOTANICAL NAME | TYPE OF PLANT |
|---|---|---|---|---|---|
| Morning glory | *Ipomoea tricolor* | annual | Rose-white blush | *Rosa* cv. | shrub |
| Mountain Laurel | *Kalmia latifolia* | shrub | Rose-white cherokee | *Rosa* cv. | shrub |
| Oleander | *Thevitica* sp. | tropical/houseplant | Rose-York & Lancaster | *Rosa damascena versicolor* | shrub |
| Oregon grape | *Mahonia aquifolium* | shrub | Rose-Provence | *Rosa centifolia* | shrub |
| Paulonia | *Pawlonia tomentosum* | tree | Rudbeckia | *Rudbeckia hirta* | perennial |
| Peach-Indian | *Prunus persica* cv. | fruit | Salvia | *Salvia officinalis* | perennial |
| Pear | *Pyrus communis* cv. | fruit | Shad bush | *Amelanchier canadensis* | perennial |
| Peony | *Paeonia officinalis* | perennial | Silk Tree | *Albizzia julibrissin* | perennial |
| Periwinkle | *Vinca minor* | perennial | Silver bell | *Halesia carolina* | perennial |
| Phlox | *Phlox* sp. | perennial | Smokebush | *Cotinus coggygria* | tree |
| Pine | *Pinus strobus* | tree | Snapdragon | *Antirrhinum majalis* | tree |
| Poppy | *Papavar orientalis* | perennial | Snowberry | *Symphoricarpos albus* | tree |
| Quince | *Cydonia oblonga* or *Chaenomeles japonica* | shrub | Snowdrops | *Galanthus nivalis* | tree |
| Rhododendron | *Rhododendron catawba & R. maximum* | shrub | Spirea | *Spiraea* sp. | tree |
|  |  |  | Spruce | *Picea glauca* | tree |
| Rose-Baltimore | *Belle Rosa* cv. *Baltimore Belle* | vine | Strawberry Bush | *Euonymus americana* | shrub |
| Rose-cabbage | *Rosa centifolia* | shrub | Sunflowers | *Helianthus annuus* | annual |
| Rose-climbing | *Rosa* cv. | vine | Sweet alyssum | *Lobularia maritima* | annual |
| Rose-damask | *Rosa damascena* | shrub | Sweet corn | *Zea maze* | biennial |
| Rose-double white | *Rosa alba* | shrub | Sweet William | *Dianthus barbatu* | biennial |
| Rose-moss | *Rosa centifolia muscosa* | shrub | Sweetshrub | *Calycanthus floridus* | shrub |
| Rose-pink damask | *Rosa damascena* | shrub | Tiger lily | *Lilium Catesbaei* | bulb |
| Rose-prairie | *Rosa setigera* | shrub | Tulip tree | *Liriodendron tulipifera* | tree |
| Rose-raspberry |  | shrub | Weeping mulberry | *Morus alba pendula* | shrub |
| Rose-red button |  | shrub | Weeping spruce | *Picea glauca pendula* | tree |
| Rose-Red damask | *Rosa damascena* | shrub | Winged euonymus | *Euonymus alata* | shrub |
| Rose-safrano | *Rosa 'Safrano'* | shrub | Wisteria | *Wisteria chinensis* | vine |
| Rose-scotch | *Rosa spinosissima* | shrub | Woodbine | *Parthenocissus quinquefolia* | vine |
| Rose-tea | *Rosa* cv. | shrub | Yew | *Taxus* | shrub |
| Rose-white | *Rosa alba* | shrub | Zinnia | *Zinnia elegans* | annual |

# Photography and Image Credits

All color photographs by Sally R. Chandler except as noted.

Photographs Courtesy of Dr. Marc Cendron and Jennifer Day, end paper opposite page 1, page 10, page 45, page 79 [top and bottom], page 80 [top], page 81, page 82 [bottom].

Photographs Courtesy of the Society for Preservation of New England Antiquities, page 73 [top, photograph by George E. Noyes], page 74 [c1899], page 76, page 108 [top 1860s, stereo-view, H.P Macintosh], page 126 [Ancient Communities and Buildings collection].

Photographs and Images, Courtesy of the Historical Society of Old Newbury, page 25, page 51 [right], page 52 [top], pages 90 and 91, page 151

Painting, page 113, Courtesy of the Colonial Williamsburg Foundation.

Photographs and Images, Courtesy of the Newburyport Public Library, page 6, page 21, page 49, page 55 [bottom], page 83, page 106, page 108 [bottom], page 121, page 123 [top], page 130 [all], page 135 [left].

Photographs from *Old Newburyport Houses* by Albert Hale, 1912, page 42 [top], page 69.

Photographs Courtesy of Mr. and Mrs. Christopher L. Snow, page 24, page 46, page 100, page 105, page 109, page 114 [bottom], back end papers.

Photographs Courtesy of the Newburyport Garden Club, front end papers, page 31 [top left and right, bottom right], page 37 [bottom], page 41 [bottom middle], page 44, page 53 [all], page 56, page 62, page 65 [top], page 77, page 82 [top], page 85 [top], page 103 [top], page 114 [top], page 155 [left and right].

Photographs by Lucinda A. Brockway, page 60, page 67, page 70, 71, page 88, page 92, page 96 [top], page 150, page 153, page 154.

Photographs Courtesy of Lucinda A. Brockway, page 41 [bottom right], page 99 [top and bottom], page 101, 102 [all], page 112 [bottom].

Photographs and images from *Gardens of Colony and State*, Garden Club of America, Alice G.B. Lockwood, 1931, Page 37 [top, plan drawn by William Perry], page 73 [bottom].

Photographs Courtesy of Jim and Sally Chandler, page 50, page 125 [top and bottom].

Photograph Courtesy of John P. Learned, page 97.

Photographs and images from *History of Newburyport, Mass* by John J. Currier 1906, Page 17 [bottom], page 19, page 29.

Photographs and plans Courtesy of the Library of Congress, Historical American Buildings Survey collection, page 39, page 40, page 47, page 57, page 59, page 63 [top and bottom], page 64 [both], page 65 [bottom].

Photographs Courtesy of Virginia Lowell, page 104, page 118, page 124, page 155 [top].

Photographs Courtesy of Elizabeth Singleton, page 103 [bottom], page 119.

Image Courtesy of the Atkinson family, page 119.

Photographs from *The Mentor* magazine, June 15, 1916, page 15 [bottom], page 42 [bottom], page 80 [bottom].

**Art Work**

Paintings Courtesy of Jennifer Day, artist, pages 32 and 33, *Cushing Carriage House*, and pages 146 and 147, *Leggy Boxwood*, Moulton house gardens.

Painting Courtesy of Lee Rowan, artist, pages 12 and 13, *Wheelwright Summerhouse*.

Pastel Courtesy of Jim and Sally Chandler, page 18, *Chain Bridge*, by F. H. Richardson, Page 98, *Dexter House Cupola*, silk screen poster by Robert Preston, 1985.

Pastel Courtesy of Gayden W. Morrill, pages 116 and 117, *Garden at 209 High Street*, by Frances R. Morrill.

Pastel Courtesy of Dennis Radulski, pages 132 and 133, *High Street Garden with Wisteria*, by Herbert Everett.

# Bibliography

Benes, Peter, ed. Plants and People. Volume 20 of Annual Proceedings of the Dublin Seminar for New England Folklife. 24 and 25 June 1995, Boston University, 1996.

Blumenson, John J. *Identifying American Architecture: A Pictorial Guide to Styles and Terms*, 1600–1945. Nashville TN: American Association for State and Local History, 1979.

Bixby, Grace. "Some gardens and flowers of yesterday." Unpublished paper. Newburyport, MA 1953.

Bradford Associates. *Master Plan Report for Atkinson Common. Prepared for the Belleville Improvement Society, Newburyport, Massachusetts.* Providence, RI: Bradford Associates, Landscape Architects, 25 Creighton Street, Providence, RI 02906, November, 1999.

City Directory for Newburyport. 1849, 1852.

Coffin, Catherine and Frank Dalton. "*The Frog Pond.*" Newburyport, MA.: City Improvement Society of Newburyport, 1975.

Currier, John J. *History of Newburyport Massachusetts.* Newburyport, Mass: Self published, 1906.

Cushing, Caleb. *The History and Present State of the Town of Newburyport.* Newburyport: E.W. Allen, 1826.

Cushing, Lemuel, *Genealogy of the Cushing Family.* Lemuel Cushing. Lovell Printing and Publishing Co. Montreal, 1877.

Emery, Sarah Anna. *Reminiscences of a Nonagenarian.* Newburyport MA: W. H. Huse, 1879.

Hale, Albert. *Old Newburyport Houses.* Boston: W.B. Clarke Co., 1912

Harvard University Archives.

Historic American Buildings Survey drawings, (HABS). Library of Congress. Recorded 1936.

Historical Society of Old Newbury Archives.

Howells, John Mead, *The Architectural Heritage of the Merrimack*, Architectural Book Publishing Company, Inc., 1941

Labaree, Benjamin W. Ed. *Samuel McIntire: A Bicentenial Symposium*, 1757–1957. Salem, Massachusetts: The Essex Institute, 1957.

Unpublished paper, "A Newburyport Friendship: Jonathan Jackson and John Lowell"

Leiner, Frederick C. *Millions for Defense: The Subscription Warships of 1798.* Naval Institute Press, Annapolis, Maryland. 2000.

McAlester, Virginia and Lee. *A Field Guide to American Houses.* New York. Alfred A. Knopf, 1991.

Moulton family private collection. Unpublished papers: List of roses in Miss Cushing's garden; Memo: re Cushing House peach tree.

National Trust for Historic Preservation Publication *Gazebos and Trellises: Authentic Details for Design and Restoration*, Peter Joel Harrison, 1999, John Wiley & Sons/Preservation Press.

Newburyport Garden Club Archives.

Northend, Mary H. *The Mentor: Historic Gardens of New England.* Serial No. 109. Volume 4, Number 9. Department of Natural History. June 15, 1916.

Perry, Shaw, Hepburn and Dean office archives.

Pierson, William H. *American Buildings and their Architects, The Colonial and Neoclassical Styles.* Garden City, New York: Anchor Books, Anchor Press/Doubleday, 1976.

Robb, David M. and J.J. Garrison. *Art in the Western World.* New York: Harper and Brothers Publishers, 1953.

Shurcliff, Arthur. "*Gardens of Old Salem and the New England Colonies.*" Essay included in *Colonial Gardens: The Landscape and Architecture of George Washington's Time.* Washington D.C.: George Washington Bicentennial Commission, 1932.

Smith, Mrs. E. Vale, *History of Newburyport.* Newburyport, 1854. Reprinted, Higginson Book Company.

Tagney, Ronald N. *The World Turned Upside Down, Essex County During America's Turbulent Years, 1763 – 1790.* Massachusetts: Essex County History, 1989.

Wakefield, Karen. "Bartlet Mall, Newburyport, Massachusetts." Unpublished paper. Newburyport, MA. 1995.

Wright, Conrad Edick, ed. *Massachusetts and the New Nation.* Massachusetts Historical Society. Boston, 1992.

*Oral Interviews:*
Clement Armstrong, Ruth Burke, Julia Farwell-Clay, Susan Heersink, Gregory Laing, Lorna Learned, Jerry Lischke, Wilhelmina and Sylvia Lunt, Beverly MacBurnie, Esther Macomber, Frank Forrest Morrill, Lillian Newbert, Maura Perkins, Christopher Snow, Jamie Yalla.

# INDEX